WALKS FOR ALL AGES
SCOTTISH BORDERS

D1344865

WALKS *FOR*
ALL AGES

SCOTTISH BORDERS

HUGH TAYLOR & MOIRA McCROSSAN

BRADWELL
BOOKS

Published by Bradwell Books
9 Orgreave Close Sheffield S13 9NP
Email: books@bradwellbooks.co.uk

1st Edition

ISBN: 9781909914346

Print: Gomer Press, Llandysul, Ceredigion SA44 4JL

Design by: Erik Siewko Creative, Derbyshire.
eriksiewko@gmail.com

Photograph Credits: © Hugh Taylor & Moira McCrossan
Front cover photograph © Walter Baxter and licensed
for reuse under the Creative Commons Licence.
iStock, Shutterstock & Creative Commons credited separately.

Maps: Contain Ordnance Survey data
© Crown copyright and database right 2014

Ordnance Survey licence number 100039353

The information in this book has been produced in good faith and is intended as a general guide. Bradwell Books and its authors have made all reasonable efforts to ensure that the details are correct at the time of publication. Bradwell Books and the author cannot accept any responsibility for any changes that have taken place subsequent to the book being published. It is the responsibility of individuals undertaking any of the walks listed in this publication to exercise due care and consideration for the health and wellbeing of each other in the party. Particular care should be taken if you are inexperienced. The walks in this book are not especially strenuous but individuals taking part should ensure they are fit and able to complete the walk before setting off.

WALKS FOR ALL AGES

INTRODUCTION

THE SCOTTISH BORDERS IS A QUIET, SECLUDED AREA, TUCKED OUT OF THE WAY IN THE SOUTH-EASTERN CORNER OF SCOTLAND. YOU MIGHT PASS THROUGH THE BORDERS AS YOU TRAVEL ALONG THE A1 OR BY TRAIN ON THE EAST COAST LINE. THERE ARE FEW MAJOR ROADS; NO LARGE TOWNS AND CERTAINLY NO CITIES. IT IS A QUIET BACKWATER OF ROLLING HILLS, COUNTRY ROADS AND PICTURESQUE TOWNS.

It was not always so; the Border area has seen more warfare and battles than most of the rest of Scotland. The Roman invasion has left traces at Newsteads, and border raids between the English and the Scots were constant for centuries. As a result you will find defensive towers, sometimes, like Duns Castle, built into substantial country houses with the tower at its heart, sometimes left in ruins like Hume Castle and sometimes almost intact like Newark Tower.

Despite the constant warfare over the centuries, the Borders was a wealthy area. However, the wealth was concentrated in the hands of a few families and above all the church. The Border abbeys are impressive and elegant, even as ruins. In their day, the monks would have owned much of the surrounding land and the abbeys would have been major trading posts. Often the land and church were gifted to the monks by the monarch and the abbeys were frequently the targets of invading armies. Henry VIII's forces did much damage during the Rough Wooing of the 1540s, followed in the next century by Oliver Cromwell. Several of the abbeys survived in use, becoming Church of Scotland parish churches after the Reformation. Coldingham Priory is still the parish church today.

The past is also evident in the small historic towns, with their market squares, narrow cobbled wynds, ancient bridges, churches and civic buildings. You may think that you have stepped thirty or forty years into a time warp, where every town would have its independent hardware shop, greengrocer, gents' outfitter, toy shop and many more. Surrounding each town and village you will find a landscape of gentle hills, rivers and forests, where you can lose yourself in the beauty and tranquillity.

Shutterstock / Dariusz Gora

COCKBURNSPATH

A PLEASANT CIRCULAR WALK TO THE COAST VIA COVE; ON SECTIONS OF THE JOHN MUIR WAY, THE SOUTHERN UPLAND WAY AND THE JAMES HUTTON WALK.

This walk starts from the 16th-century Mercat Cross, beside the car park. You'll notice carved emblems of a thistle on two of the faces and roses on the other two. This was the marriage of the Thistle and the Rose, in 1503, when James IV of Scotland married Margaret Tudor, daughter of Henry VII of England. The marriage was the final seal on the Treaty of Perpetual Peace between England and Scotland and Cockburnspath formed part of the dowry given by James to his new wife. Unfortunately peace didn't last long and James, together with the bulk of the Scottish nobility, was killed at Flodden in 1513. But because of this marriage James VI of Scotland succeeded Elizabeth I of England to become James I of England in the Union of Crowns in 1603.

Cockburnspath is at the eastern end of the Southern Upland Way (SUW), a rather strenuous long-distance footpath that crosses southern Scotland from Portpatrick on the west coast. Because it is cutting across the grain of the land it involves a considerable amount of ascent and descent. Long stretches of moorland and a lack of suitable overnight accommodation mean that far fewer people attempt this route than the more popular West Highland Way. Nevertheless it has a lot to offer, as you will find on this short stretch, which is not at all taxing. The John Muir Way originally ran from Musselburgh to Cockburnspath. In 2014 it was expanded to become a long-distance coast-to-coast route starting from Dunbar. The section you will be walking on has been renamed The John Muir Link. Muir, who was born in Dunbar in 1838, is generally regarded as the father of the American National Parks.

James Hutton was an East Lothian farmer whose observations and research laid the foundation of modern geological theory and proved conclusively that the Earth was more than just a few thousand years old. Siccar Point, which is a couple of miles south of Cove, is where you can go to see Hutton's Unconformity, where sloping strata of Devonian Old Red Sandstone, formed 334 million years ago, overlie almost vertical layers of 425-million-year-old Silurian greywacke.

THE BASICS

Distance: 3¾ miles / 6km
Gradient: Some short inclines but mainly flat level going
Severity: Easy
Approx time to walk: 2 hrs
Stiles: None
Maps: OS Explorers 346 (Berwick-upon-Tweed) and 351 (Dunbar and North Berwick)
Path description: Mainly on footpaths, some surfaces and a short road section
Start point: Centre of Cockburnspath at Mercat Cross (GR NT 774711)
Parking: In the village square next to the Mercat Cross (TD13 5YX)
Landscape: Woodland, pasture, coastline
Dog friendly: A good walk for dogs
Public toilets: Downhill from the start. You pass them towards the end of the walk
Nearest food: There is a community café in the village hall on Wednesdays
Otherwise head to Eyemouth (15 miles) or Dunbar (8 miles)

COCKBURNSPATH WALK

1. Facing the Mercat Cross turn right onto Callander Place, then go past the primary school to continue onto a grassy footpath by a finger post indicating that this is the John Muir Way to Dunbar. Go through a gate and keep on. To your left is woodland but over to the right the ground slopes away and the views are magnificent.

2. When the woodland ends continue to contour round the hill, following the path, to go through a gate into the woods. Turn right onto a forest road and continue downhill to reach a T-junction with the main road. Turn left onto it, cross a bridge, then turn left onto a lane heading up hill to visit Dunglass Collegiate Church.

3. Return to the road, cross over, and head down a lane in the direction indicated by the John Muir Way finger post. Go under a railway

viaduct, turn right onto a footpath and continue on it, downhill, passing under two further bridges. When the path reaches a junction, leave the John Muir Way and turn right.

4. Cross the Old Dunglass Bridge. Continue along a footpath through woodland to reach a T-junction with a metalled road. Turn right onto it. Follow it until it reaches the roundabout at the A1 then keep left, on the pavement, cross the road and continue on the pavement opposite heading towards Cove.

5. When the pavement ends turn left across the road and then down a narrower road, into the village of Cove and follow this to reach the car park. From here continue on the Southern Upland Way. This section is also part of the James Hutton Walk (Border Brains Walks). When the path turns right, at the end of some houses, keep ahead, and pass a gate to continue along the coast.

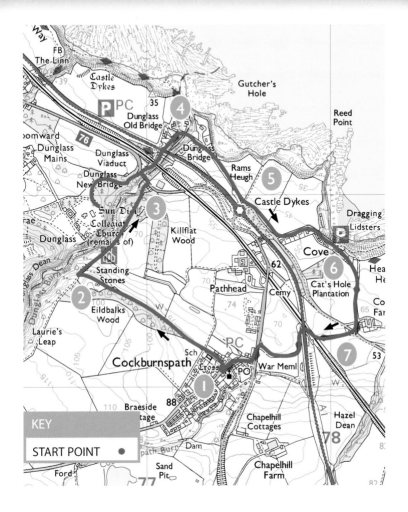

6. When you reach a path junction, by a finger post, turn right and continue on a grassy path that follows the line of a fence. When this reaches some buildings, cross a track and continue on the way-marked SUW on another track that passes to the right of a house. When this reaches a T-junction with a road, turn left, then immediately right onto a rough road that passes in front of a row of cottages.

7. Continue following the SUW from here, go under a railway bridge, turn right, and then left under a road bridge. Keep on this path following way-markers until it reaches the main road in Cockburnspath at a T-junction. Turn left then right after the Cockburnspath Garage to return to the village square.

ST ABB'S HEAD

THIS IS A FASCINATING IF ENERGETIC WALK ALONG A SPECTACULAR COASTLINE, TO A LIGHTHOUSE THROUGH AN AREA OF ABUNDANT WILDLIFE.

St Abb's was named for Aebbe, who, from 643 to her death around 680, was abbess of a monastery, traces of which can still be seen on Kirk Hill. The craggy coastline of St Abb's Head, formed by ancient volcanic eruptions, is a National Nature Reserve and a paradise for birdwatchers, walkers and wildlife lovers.

From the cliffs you can see thousands of nesting seabirds, including guillemots, kittiwakes and razorbills. On the stacks offshore look for guillemots massed together and razorbills nesting in single pairs or small groups. You will need to look hard for puffins as there are only a few pairs nesting in crevices in the cliff. The kittiwakes are found near the lighthouse in grass and mud nests on the cliff face, while shags and herring gulls nest on low, flat rocks. It is well worth taking along a pocket bird book to identify all the different birds wheeling around these cliffs. Look out to sea too for a glimpse of the harbour porpoise, a small dolphin that you may see on a calm day. The whole coast here is part of a European Marine Site and many sub aqua divers are attracted to explore the abundant sea life in the clean waters.

The cliffs are colourful with sea campion and other plants tolerant of salt spray and wind. A little inland there are more birds to be observed as meadow pipits, linnets and black and grey wheatears thrive on the abundant seeds and insect life. In the Mire Loch there are eels, perch and sticklebacks as well as frogs and toads.

The valley of the Mire Loch is also on the line of the St Abb's Head fault, separating two different kinds of rock. You can quite clearly see the difference. As you look to the west you see sedimentary rocks, deposited as layers of mud around 450 million years ago and gradually pushed and squeezed into mountains by the movements of the Earth's crust.

Over millions of years they have been worn down into the rounded shapes you see today. To the east you can see the rugged lava that erupted from volcanoes around 400 million years ago. The lava is more resistant to erosion so in time St Abb's Head will probably become an island.

Shutterstock / tjwvandongen

THE BASICS

Distance: 3½ miles / 6km
Gradient: Up and down most of the way with a few long climbs
Severity: Moderate
Approx time to walk: 2 hrs
Stiles: One but there is an alternative path around it
Map: OS Explorer 346 (Berwick-upon-Tweed)
Path description: Cliff paths, hill tracks and country lanes
Start point: National Trust for Scotland Car Park at St Abb's (GR NT914675)
Parking: Car park (TD14 5QF)
Landscape: Coast and hill
Dog friendly: Dog friendly walk, on leads near livestock
Public toilets: Car park
Nearest food: Old Smiddy Tearoom at the National Trust Centre

ST ABB'S HEAD WALK

1. Take the path from the car park that leads to the National Trust Centre. Walk along the front of the buildings, pass them then veer off the path, over the grass and through a gate onto the road. Turn left and then immediately left again onto a footpath that runs parallel to the road. Follow this a short distance until it meets a wall then turn left, following the sign pointing to the 'Footpath to St Abb's Head'.

2. The path runs alongside a high wall to go through a gate, then turns left at a picnic table and heads uphill following the cliff edge. It's important to stay away from the edge of the cliff, and if you are walking with young children keep a firm grip on them. Take it easy on the short climb from here to the top of the cliff. There's a strategically placed bench where you can take a well-earned rest.

3. Follow the narrow coastal path as it winds along. But stop often to take photographs and to enjoy the views. Behind you is the small fishing village and harbour of St Abb's. You can also see one of the bronze memorials by Jill Watson commemorating the women and children left behind by the East Coast Fishing Disaster. The path continues over grass. When it forks near a small knoll, keep left and head downhill, descending stone steps to walk along the edge of a bay.

4. From here the path veers away from the coast and crosses a field to reach a gate just after a short climb. Go through this and continue on the path to reach a fenced in area where you may be fortunate to catch sight of the Brown Argus Butterfly in the summer months. Shortly after this you will reach a finger post pointing ahead for the Coastal Path.

5. If you do not want to do the full walk you can turn left here and follow this grassy path to the bottom of the loch, going through two gates to where it meets the return leg of the full walk at point 8. But there is much to be seen by continuing and although it's a wee bit of a climb it is manageable by anyone of reasonable fitness. The secret is to go slowly and take short steps. Move at a speed where you are able to maintain a conversation.

6. Keep ahead on a grassy path that heads uphill beside the fence. When you reach the top you have to head back down the other side only to find another climb in front of you. Eventually you will see the top of the lighthouse peeping over the horizon, then the keepers' cottages. One last climb takes you up to them. Pass to the left of the buildings and in a short distance head down stone steps to reach the tarmac road.

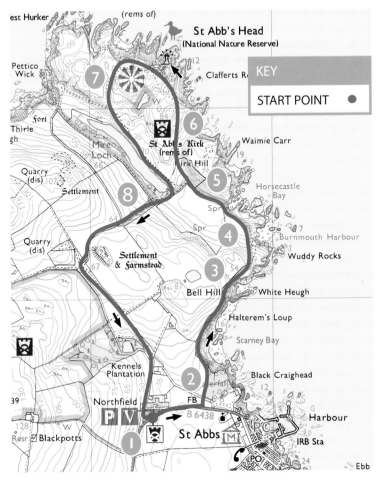

7. Head along this and eventually you will see the loch below you on the left. As the road starts to turn right, turn left just before the metal barrier and head downhill on a rough footpath. There's a short steep descent and then when the path forks, go right to reach the lower path by the loch side. Continue on this and when the path forks again keep ahead. Eventually arrive at the dam at the head of the loch.

8. Head downhill then turn right to cross a plank bridge, up some steps, left over a stile and walk across the dam and then rejoin the path; or to avoid the stile continue on the path, although this misses the lovely view from the dam down the length of the loch. Follow the path uphill to go through a gate and onto a quiet country lane. Follow this all the way back to the car park.

COLDINGHAM PRIORY

This walk takes you from a ruined priory to possibly the best beach in the Borders and returns by an ancient route for fishermen.

The name Coldingham is derived from a place named urbs Coludi or Colud's fort, mentioned by the first English historian, Bede in the early 700s. Coldingham Priory was founded in 1098 by King Edgar of Scotland, the son of Malcolm Canmore and St Margaret, as thanksgiving to God for recovering his kingdom from Donald Bane, his uncle, who had usurped it at his father's death. He granted the land to Benedictine monks from Durham and established a church there in 1100. However, the first prior is not recorded until 1147. The

information in the Luckenbooth, at the priory entrance, and the panels throughout the site bring its history to life. In the grounds, look out for the carved stone inscriptions suggested by local schoolchildren. The interior of the church contains surviving 14th-century stone carving from the original Priory. Although it was rebuilt several times over the centuries, the monastery was largely destroyed by Oliver Cromwell in 1648, but the remains of the choir are still in use as the Church of Scotland parish church of Coldingham.

Coldingham Bay lies about a mile from the village on this walk. The beach is only about 200 yards wide and is sheltered by rocky headlands to the north and south of the sands. An unusual feature is the line of colourful beach huts, some of which are believed to be 100 years old. The beach is popular with surfers and body boarders, taking advantage of huge rolling white waves. Children will love dipping in the pools along the rocky shore, where they will find a huge variety of marine life. Lifeguards are on duty in summer when the beach gets very busy and there is a cafe, toilets, disabled access and car parking.

The beach has received the Seaside Award, which is for beaches that are more rural in character, being quieter and less developed. The Marine Conservation Society has also awarded the beach the top award for cleanliness every year since 2006 and in 2010 the beach was awarded the prestigious Blue Flag, which is based on a wide range of criteria, including water quality, facilities, safety and environmental features.

The return part of this walk is along the ancient Creel Path. This has been a thoroughfare for over a thousand years. The local fishermen who lived in Fisher's Brae in Coldingham used it to reach their boats on what was Coldingham Shore and is now St Abbs.

THE BASICS

Distance: 2¾ miles / 4.5km
Gradient: Some uphill stretches and steps but mainly flat level going
Severity: Easy
Approx time to walk: 1½ hrs
Stiles: None
Map: OS Explorer 346 (Berwick-upon-Tweed)
Path description: Quiet roads, boardwalk and paths
Start point: Coldingham Priory car park (GR NT904660)
Parking: Car park (TD14 5NL)
Landscape: Village, fields, beach and cliff
Dog friendly: Yes
Public toilets: Car park and Coldingham Beach
Nearest food: Coldingham, Luckenbooth at car park

COLDINGHAM PRIORY WALK

1. Leave the car park and turn right onto the High Street, following signs for Coldingham Bay, Stoutcraft Caravan Park and Head Start Coffee Shop. As you pass along High Street keep a look out on your right for a blue plaque on the house where pioneering photographer John Wood lived. An archive of 600 of his glass negatives from the early 20th century was discovered in 1992 and you can look at some of them later in Coldingham Luckenbooth.

2. Just past the Spar shop turn left into Christison's Brae and head downhill to the ford. Turn right at the ford along the boardwalk and then a path to a wooden bridge. Cross the bridge and continue with the burn on your right until you go up some steps and emerge at a gravel road.

3. Continue on the gravel road to a crossroads with the main road. Cross the road and continue ahead on the road to Coldingham Bay. Look out for a footpath sign for Coldingham Bay, turn left and go onto a footpath that runs parallel to the road and behind a hedge. Keep on this heading downhill towards the sea until it ends. Then continue in the same direction along the road, passing the beach car park.

4. At the end of the road a signpost directs you to go left onto the footpath for Coldingham Beach. Almost immediately turn right and head downhill on the path to the beach, passing public toilets to reach a finger post. Turn left here following the coastal path to St Abbs. This passes along the front of some gaily painted beach huts then turns right, down some steps and onto the beach.

5. Turn left and head along the beach, keeping a sharp lookout for stone steps heading uphill on the left. A finger post part way up will confirm you are on the right steps. Halfway up there is a convenient bench if you need a rest. As you emerge out of woodland onto the cliff path near a memorial bench there is a finger post. Turn left here on the Link to Creel Path.

6. This heads uphill following the line of a wall. There are great views over Coldingham Bay. Shortly turn right at a yellow way-marker onto a grassy path

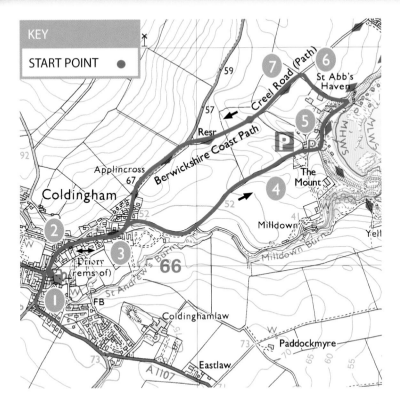

through a garden, passing to the right of a house. Continue on the path to reach a T-junction with a finger post. Turn left here onto the Creel Road. This was the route that the fishermen from Coldingham took to and from St Abbs shore. Pass a junction with a finger post and keep straight ahead.

7. When you reach a T-junction with the road turn left and follow it back past the crossroads to Fishers' Brae, previously called Cadgers Hill because it ran to Coldingham Shore for the cadgers or fish merchants. Look for a road to the left signposted for the Chariot Road and follow it to some gates. Turn right here along the Chariot Road, which brings you to the back of the Priory. There are several gates to enter by and you can explore the grounds of the Priory and then make your way back to the car park.

EYEMOUTH HARBOUR

ENJOY THE BUSTLE OF A HISTORIC WORKING HARBOUR, FEED THE SEALS AND EXPLORE AN OLD FORT WITH REAL CANNONS.

The narrow streets and vennels of Eyemouth are exactly what you would expect in a traditional village, where fishing was the core of the local economy. The infamous Eyemouth disaster of October 1881, known locally as Black Friday, took the lives of 129 Eyemouth fishermen. In a sudden violent storm many boats capsized, while others were dashed to pieces on the rocks.

For the full story and to see the magnificent tapestry commemorating the disaster, visit Eyemouth Museum. The memorial to those who lost their lives and also a poignant bronze of women and children looking out to sea are in the old cemetery between High Street and Albert Road.

Fishing was undoubtedly the main industry of Eyemouth but another more clandestine trade was plied on the seas. Eyemouth is the closest Scottish port to the Continent, so it was inevitably attractive to smugglers. Brandy, tobacco and tea were highly taxed and so smuggling was an extremely profitable, if dangerous, trade. There were hiding places and secret passages everywhere in the town. The famous smuggler John Nisbet built Gunsgreen House in 1753 with lots of hidden spaces to hide his smuggled goods. Supposedly there were hiding places for smuggled goods built into the walls between rooms, and even a fireplace which swung open. Gunsgreen House, designed by James Adam of the famous Adam architectural family, is now a fun and interactive museum of smuggling.

Eyemouth's geographical position also made it an important strategic point, which is why the fort was built. It was built in two phases, first by the English in 1547 as part of Henry VIII's 'Rough Wooing' to marry his son, the future Edward VI to Mary, Queen of Scots. But that only lasted for three years before it was demolished. The main result of Henry VIII's campaign was to drive the Scots closer to the French.

The young Mary, Queen of Scots was sent to France to be betrothed to the Dauphin of France and from 1557 to 1560 the fort was occupied by the French. It was finally demolished in 1559 but the extent of the fort is still visible on the point. However, don't miss the interactive 3D exhibit in Eyemouth Museum, which brings it to life as it was in the 16th century.

THE BASICS

Distance: 2 miles / 3km

Gradient: Mainly flat with one climb to the fort

Severity: Easy

Approx time to walk: 1½ hrs

Stiles: None

Map: OS Explorer 346 (Berwick-upon-Tweed)

Path description: Roads, beach, paths and harbour side

Start point: The Auld Kirk, Information Point, Manse Road (GR NT945643)

Parking: Roads alongside park (TD14 5HE)

Landscape: Streets and coastline

Dog friendly: On leads on roads and by the harbour

Public toilets: At the harbour

Nearest food: Ship Inn on the harbour and many other pubs and cafés

EYEMOUTH HARBOUR WALK

1. Start at the Auld Kirk, now a museum and visitor centre. Go along Manse Road to the harbour and turn left onto the Old Quay, which is normally a hive of activity. There may be fishing boats or leisure craft and there might be a fish stall selling fish to feed the seals. But do bear in mind, as a sign reminds you, that this is a working harbour.

2. Continue along the quay, passing the Ship Hotel and the Fishermen's Mission, turning left into Marine Parade, then continue alongside the beach on the Bantry, and look out from here to see the dangerous Hurkur Rocks, which have claimed the lives of many sailors.

3. At the end of the Bantry is a row of former coastguards' cottages. Turn right here along the beach to a set of steps leading up to the fort. At the top turn right along the cliff to explore the remains of the fort. You can walk right around here and return to the top of the steps. Make sure to see the two cannon at the end pointing out to sea.

4. From here continue along the cliff path towards the town to Fort Road. Head down Fort Road and at the end turn left into High Street, passing a fish merchant's with a small smokehouse at the back. Look out for the entrance to the old cemetery, now a garden, where you will find the memorial to those lost at sea in the Eyemouth fishing disaster and the bronze memorial to the wives and children left behind.

5. Further along there are the old Parish School and the Schoolhouse at the corner of Armatage Street and an art deco building on the right at the start of Market Place. At number 4 Market Place there is a marriage lintel dated 1735 and on number 2 there is a plaque indicating that in this lodge Robert Burns was made a Royal Arch Mason in 1787.

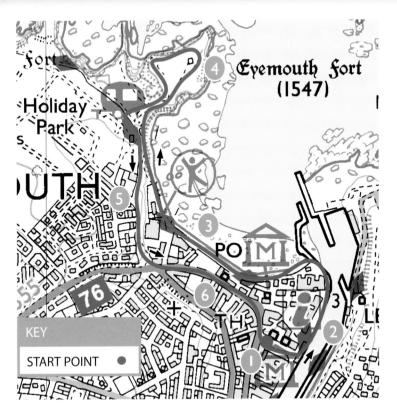

6. The Council Offices, which used to be the Commercial Bank of Scotland premises, is a grand turreted Victorian building on the right, just opposite the Auld Kirk, which brings you back to the start.

DUNS & HEN POO LAKE

AN HISTORIC BORDER TOWN, A PLEASANT WOODLAND WALK BY A LAKE FULL OF WATER LILIES AND A TURRETED MEDIAEVAL CASTLE.

The little town of Duns, like many border towns, has echoed to the sound of marching soldiers many times in its history. On one occasion in the 14th century the townspeople frightened the English horses with rattles and chased the soldiers out of town. Several times in the 16th century, the town was burnt to the ground by the English and in the 17th century both the Covenanters and Cromwell camped at Duns. In more peaceful times, particularly in the 19th century, the town expanded, so if you have time, have a wander around the historic buildings in the centre, before or after your walk.

The Market Square has the traditional Mercat Cross of Scottish towns, indicating the site of markets, fairs and general gatherings. Around the square you will see several buildings worth a closer look. There are two notable bank buildings: the elegant Royal Bank designed in 1857 and the very Scottish, early 20th-century design of the Bank of Scotland with its array of narrow windows.

The Working Men's Institute, built in 1877, has a Dutch gable with its name and date carved in the stone, above unusual pillars starting at the first-floor level. The three-storey Georgian Tolbooth, where merchants paid for their licences to trade, also served as a prison; the clock was added more recently in 1976. At the other end of the town, the Jim Clark Room charts the life and achievements of the legendary racing driver who won the Formula 1 world championship in 1963 and 1965.

On the walk, look for the cairn to John Duns Scotus on the site of his birth. He was an influential mediaeval theologian and philosopher, whose writings are still highly regarded by philosophers. However, when his arguments fell out of favour in the 16th century, his name came to be used to describe someone not very clever – a dunce.

The best view of the castle is on the return journey from the lake. The original Duns Castle dates from the 14th century, built by the Earl of Moray, the nephew of Robert the Bruce. It has been owned and added to by successive generations of the Hay family since 1696 and the architect, James Gillespie Graham, in the early 19th century, designed the transformation from peel tower to turreted Gothic castle.

THE BASICS

Distance: 3¾ miles / 6km
Gradient: Negligible
Severity: Easy
Approx time to walk: 2 hrs
Stiles: None
Map: OS Explorer 346 (Berwick-upon-Tweed)
Path description: Public roads and estate roads
Start point: Market Square, Duns (GR NT785538)
Parking: On-road parking in Duns (TD11 3BX)
Landscape: Town, woodland and lakeside
Dog friendly: Keep dogs on leads around livestock
Public toilets: Briery Baulk, off South Street, Duns
Nearest food: Several cafés around the Market Square

DUNS & HEN POO LAKE WALK

1. From the Market Square in Duns go up Castle Street. Cross the main road and continue on Castle Street. Pass Teindhillgreen and a field called Tinkers' Acre on the right and then go through North Lodge archway at the end of the street.

2. Continue on the estate road as far as Pavilion Lodge, which leads to the castle drive. Beyond this is private. Just before Pavilion Lodge on the right is a cairn commemorating the mediaeval philosopher John Duns Scotus.

3. Go right here following the estate road to Hen Poo Lake. In summer the surface of the lake is covered with a mass of water lilies and you can see swans and ducks with their cygnets and ducklings. At the end of the lake turn left and then almost immediately left again to follow a woodland path along the other side of the lake.

4. Look out about halfway along for a hide on the edge of the lake, from where you can watch the abundant wildlife of the lake. At the end of the forest at a crossroads, go straight ahead through a gate. Continue on the estate road back towards Duns, looking out to the left for views of the superb Duns Castle.

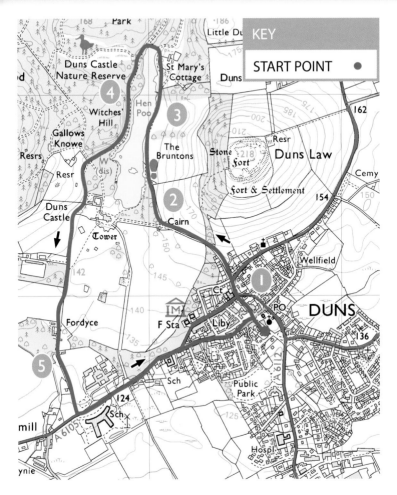

KEY

START POINT ●

5. Continue ahead until you reach the main road. Turn left passing the new Berwickshire High School on the right and the South Lodge entrance to the castle on the left. Continue along the main street to Castle Street and turn back down to Market Square.

GREENLAW & HUME CASTLE

HUME CASTLE WAS BUILT ON TOP OF A SMALL HILL DURING THE LATE 12TH CENTURY. FROM ITS BATTLEMENTS YOU CAN SEE THE ENTIRE OUTLINE OF THIS WALK AND AS FAR AWAY AS THE ENGLISH BORDER AT CARTER BAR.

Because of its strategic location it was in early use as a beacon station warning people if England invaded. This function continued long after the castle was destroyed. In 1804, when there was fear of an invasion by the French forces of Napoleon Bonaparte, a lookout mistakenly took the light from a charcoal burner's fire on Dirrington Law as another beacon and lit up the one on Hume, which in turn fired the rest of the Borders Beacons and led to what was thereafter called 'The Great Alarm' when over 3,000 volunteers turned out to repel the supposed invaders. During World War II Hume was used again as a lookout post.

Throughout its long history Hume was captured and retaken on many occasions. Even in 1313, when Robert the Bruce laid waste to the Borders as part of his scorched earth policy aimed at leaving nothing that the invading English army could use for shelter or supplies, Hume survived. It was the only Borders Castle not destroyed at that time. But by 1651 there had been significant advances in military armaments and when Cromwell's invasion force arrived at Hume their artillery fire reduced it to a ruin. It was never rebuilt.

In 1789 Hugh Hume-Campbell, the 3rd Earl of Marchmont built the present wall around what remained of the castle. It was more of a folly than a restoration and that is why the wall has huge crenellations. While it provides a rather pretty spectacle from miles around they have little practical use.

Hume is the ancestral home of the Home (pronounced 'Hume') family. They took their name from the area after the grandson of the Earl of Dunbar acquired the land some time in the 13th century. How Hume became Home is not really known but one legend has it that during the Battle of Flodden in 1513 Lord Hume adopted the battle cry 'A Home! A Home!' until he discovered that many of his troops had taken it literally and left the battlefield.

THE BASICS

Distance: 2¾ miles / 4.5km

Gradient: Slight inclines but nothing of significance

Severity: Easy

Approx time to walk: ¾ hr to 1¼ hrs

Stiles: None

Map: OS Explorer 339 (Kelso, Coldstream and Lower Tweed Valley)

Path description: Grassy tracks, country lanes and dirt tracks

Start point: Car Park at Hume Castle (GR NT705415)

Parking: At the start (TD5 7TR)

Landscape: Merse, farmland and hills

Dog friendly: Dog-friendly walk but keep on lead near livestock

Public toilets: In nearby Greenlaw, The Square (3 miles)

Nearest food: The Poppy Coffee House, Bank Street, Greenlaw (TD10 6XX)

1. Exit the Castle car park and turn left onto the road. Where the road bends, beside a way-marker to St Nicholas Church and Homebyres, keep ahead on a grassy track that runs between two drystone walls. Keep on this to reach a T-junction with another grassy track then turn left.

2. Head downhill on this track, which is a bit overgrown and can be muddy when wet, to reach the walls of the St Nicholas Cemetery. Enter via the gate and have a wander round. The foundations of the old church are at the north end of the cemetery. Hume was once a much larger parish than it is now. In the early 17th century a large part of it was transferred to Gordon parish. The church of St Nicholas was closed in 1640 and all that now remains is the outline of its foundations. Nearby you will see the burial vaults of the Earls of Home. Look out for some interesting gravestones. Propped against a tree is an ancient stone from the early 18th century. But look round the back of it where there is a relief carving of a skull and crossbones, probably from an earlier grave marker.

3. Leave the old cemetery and turn left onto the track. Follow this to a country lane, then turn left and keep on to a junction where you turn left again. Keep on this lane to reach a house on the left and a signpost pointing left to Camling and Hume Mill. Turn left onto a grassy track and follow it to a farm at the burn. The site of the old Hume

Mill is on the left and you can still see a small part of the ruins. Witches Hill is to your right.

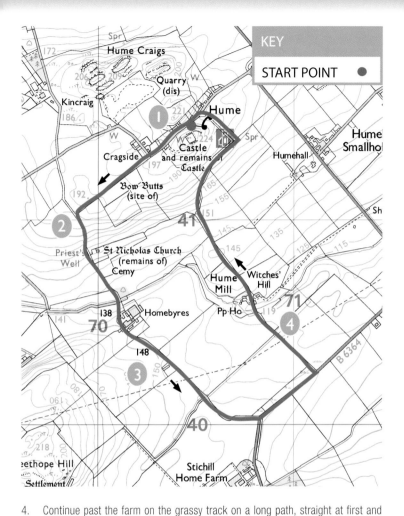

KEY

START POINT ●

4. Continue past the farm on the grassy track on a long path, straight at first and then winding up past the castle to the road. Pass through two gates on the way. The path may be boggy in parts. You will have splendid views of the castle all the way up. At the road turn left back to the car park. Go through the gate on the car park and climb up to the castle. You can climb up onto the walls of the folly and from near the flagpole you can trace the route you have just walked.

EDNAM – RULE BRITANNIA

A WALK AROUND PASTURELANDS, A MONUMENT AND ONE
OF THE BEST VIEWS IN THE BORDERS.

James Thomson was born in 1700 in Ednam,
the son of the parish minister. Born just seven
years before the Treaty of Union, he was part of
the first generation of Scots who grew up without
an independent Scottish Parliament. He studied
divinity at Edinburgh University, where he met his
lifelong friend and collaborator David Mallet. After
the successful publication of some of his poems
in the Edinburgh Miscellany, Thomson followed
Mallet to London in search of literary recognition.

In 1725 he published 'Spring', the first part of a long poem called The Seasons. It was
immediately popular, and as the other three parts followed, its success secured his fame
and popularity.

Thomson's words for 'Rule, Britannia' were written in 1740 as part of the masque, *Alfred*,
which he and Mallet wrote for Frederick, Prince of Wales. It may be that Thomson's
generation felt British in a way that Scots had not before. It was set to music by Thomas
Arne and quickly became one of the best-known British patriotic songs, developing an
independent life of its own, quite apart from the original and forgotten masque.

It became so well known that Handel quoted it in his *Occasional Oratorio* in 1846, in
the aria, 'Prophetic visions strike my eye'. Similarly, the Jacobites altered Thomson's
words to a pro-Jacobite version, '… when royal Charles by Heaven's command, arrived
in Scotland's noble Plain'. It echoed the spirit
of the age as Britain and France were at war
for much of the 18th century and the French
were undoubtedly the main example of 'haughty
tyrants', whose 'slaves' Britons should never be.

It remained popular in the 19th century, by which
time Britannia did indeed rule the waves and the
sun never set on the British Empire. Gilbert and
Sullivan used parts of 'Rule, Britannia' several
times in their comic operas, including in the finale
of *HMS Pinafore* to celebrate the jubilee of Queen
Victoria in 1887. Edward Elgar used it in several

works, including the *Enigma Variations* and it has traditionally been performed at the Last Night of the Proms. However, despite all the variations, Thomson's original words remain the best known, although his original chorus:

© Stuart Meak

Rule, Britannia! Rule the waves:
Britons never will be slaves.

has popularly changed to:

Rule Britannia!'
Britannia rule the waves
Britons never, never, never shall be slaves.

THE BASICS

Distance: 2¼ miles / 3.5km
Gradient: Mainly flat with one short hill
Severity: Easy
Approx time to walk: 1 hr to 1¼ hrs
Stiles: None
Map: OS Explorer 339 (Kelso, Coldstream and Lower Tweed Valley)
Path description: Road and grassy paths
Start point: Car park in Ednam (GR NT737372)
Parking: Car park (TD5 7PW)
Landscape: Pasture and rolling hills
Dog friendly: On lead on the road
Public toilets: Kelso, Horsemarket
Nearest food: Kelso

EDNAM WALK

1. From the car park head towards the hotel and the church and continue on the track ahead. As the road bends, turn left over a footbridge over the Eden Water and continue to the road.

2. Turn left along the B6461 and go along as far as the lodge house. You will pass the obelisk on the hill to your left. At the lodge house turn left along a quiet country lane.

3. Continue along the lane until you reach the path to the monument on your left. Take the grassy path up to the monument to James Thomson, who wrote the words of 'Rule, Britannia'. Admire the views over the surrounding countryside and retrace your steps to the road.

4. Turn left and continue along the country lane until you reach a gate on the left. Go through here and walk along the edge of the field. This was once the Ferry Road to the ferry over the Tweed near Sprouston.

5. At the road turn left to return to the bridge and retrace your steps to the car park.

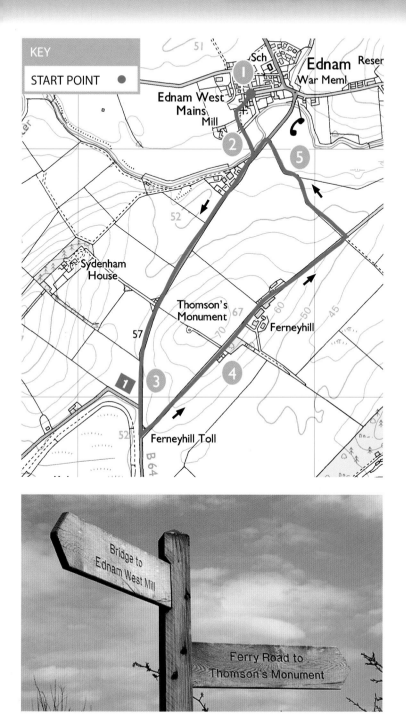

KEY

START POINT ●

KELSO

THIS WALK TAKES IN KELSO'S TWO MAIN BRIDGES, BUILT ALMOST TWO CENTURIES APART, AND THE TOWN'S FAMOUS ABBEY.

David I, King of Scots, 1124–1153, is credited with introducing the feudal system from England and encouraging Norman families to settle here and become local rulers. Those that accepted his invitation built great castles in Berwick, Selkirk and Jedburgh. David also created a series of Royal Burghs with trading privileges aimed at developing the country's economy and established a Scottish coinage by creating royal mints in Berwick and Roxburgh. He also founded the great Border abbeys. The first of these was built at Selkirk around 1119. This subsequently moved to its current location by 1128, possibly due to King David having created the Royal Burgh of Roxburgh as a major economic and administrative centre.

The abbey was constructed by a community of Tironensian monks from Tiron Abbey near Chartres in France. The income it collected from its vast border estates made it the wealthiest abbey in Scotland. What had been a mere clachan, a small settlement, before the abbey was built developed into the prosperous town of Kelso. This was the largest of the abbeys and it was here that the nine-year-old King James III was crowned in 1460 after his father was killed when cannon exploded while he was besieging nearby Roxburgh Castle to regain it from the English.

Because of its proximity to the border the area was frequently attacked and occupied during the 14th century by English forces. After each attack the monks set about rebuilding and repairing damage. The next century was more settled but by the 16th century it came under attack again. During the Rough Wooing (see Walk 4, Eyemouth) in the 1540s Henry VIII's forces inflicted heavy damage on all of the abbeys.

© Jim Barton

Then in 1560, at the Scottish Reformation, the monastic communities were disestablished and no longer recognised. There were more attacks on the building, which was officially declared derelict in 1587. By the early 17th century the estates had been transferred to secular control under the last Commendator of the abbey, Robert Ker of Cessford. Part of the ruins continued to be used as a parish kirk until the late 18th century, while other sections were demolished and the stone was recycled for buildings in Kelso. In 1805 lots of the ruins were cleared along with the kirk. Only the west tower and transept now remain.

THE BASICS

Distance: 2 miles / 3km

Gradient: A few sets of steps and a couple of slight gradients

Severity: Easy

Approx time to walk: ¾ hr to 1¼ hrs

Stiles: None

Map: OS Explorer 339 (Kelso, Coldstream and Lower Tweed Valley)

Path description: Mainly pavements and footpaths, some muddy sections

Start point: Council Car Park at The Butts (GR NT728338)

Parking: At start (TD5 7BA)

Landscape: Town, riverside, woodland

Dog friendly: A good dog walk

Public toilets: At Croft Park beside the Edinburgh Road, A6089

Nearest food: Several options are available in the town square

KELSO WALK

1. It is well worth taking some time to explore the abbey either before you go or when you return from your walk. From the abbey car park, follow the path across the green to Kelso Square and go to the south-west corner and down Bridge Street, past the Ednam House Hotel on the right. Pause for a moment to admire this fine Georgian townhouse built in 1761. On the left The Queen's Head Hotel is a coaching house of the same period.

2. Pass the abbey on the left and continue along to pass the war memorial and then cross Rennie's Bridge. This was built in the early 19th century and opened in 1803. John Rennie from Haddington designed it and a few years later used the same design for Waterloo Bridge in London. Rennie also designed the more famous London Bridge, which was ultimately dismantled and replaced in 1967. An American bought the old bridge and later rebuilt in Arizona. The two iron lamp standards on the far end of the bridge were rescued from Waterloo Bridge and re-erected here.

3. Just past the lamps turn left down some steps. This brings you into Bridgend Park. Go straight through the park to the Millennium Viewpoint at the exit, which affords a fine view of the town.

4. Turn left from here along Maxwell Heugh. Shortly turn left into Sprouston Street. Look out for a gate lodge on your left. Turn into the drive at the lodge and then left again through a wooden gate. Go through woodland and down some steps to reach the Tweed.

5. Go along the river bank and up some steps to a small park. Turn left into the housing estate and at a T-junction turn right and then left and left again onto the B6350.

6. Continue downhill towards the Hunter Bridge. Before you reach the bridge look for a path on your right up to the road. When you reach the road turn left and cross the bridge. Go straight ahead to the roundabout and cross into Sheddon Park.

7. Cross the park and come out close to another roundabout. Turn right to the roundabout and then left into Horsemarket. Follow Horsemarket back to the Square and retrace your steps to the Abbey.

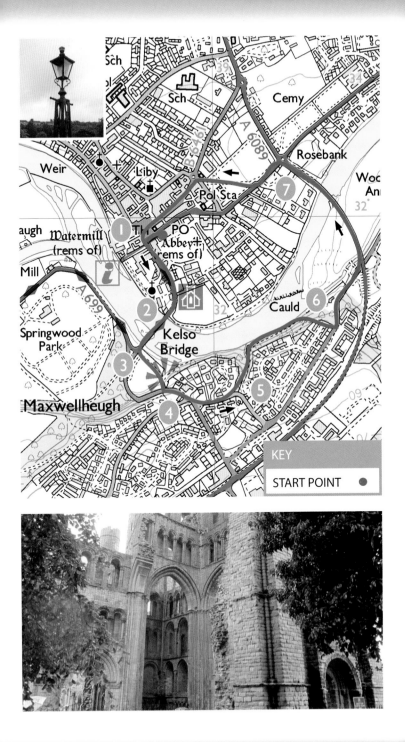

KEY

START POINT ●

KIRK YETHOLM

WALK FROM THE PENNINE WAY ONTO THE ST CUTHBERT'S
WAY AND A COUNTRY ROAD TO COMPLETE A CIRCUIT OF
TWO SMALL VILLAGES AND MANY CENTURIES OF SCOTTISH
HISTORY.

A few hundred yards' walk along the Pennine Way from the start of the walk will take you to the famous Gypsy Palace. The King or Queen of the Gypsies lived on this spot for nearly 300 years. The last King was crowned here in 1898 and although the Gypsies have now all but vanished some of their traditions live on. In Town Yetholm two young people are chosen each year to be the Bari Gadgi and Bari Manushi (Romany for best boy and best girl) during the village festival in June.

Johnny Faa was the traditional name of the Gypsy King. In 1540 King James IV issued him with a letter under the Privy Seal recognising him as 'lord and earl of Little Egypt' and granting him authority over all of the Gypsies who had to conform to Gypsy law. Even so it was not easy being a Gypsy in Scotland and they were expelled in 1541 and again in 1609. Various men called Johnny Faa were hung for returning to the country in 1611, 1616 and 1624.

The most famous legend attached to Johnny Faa is preserved in an ancient ballad that has many variations. It's based on the legend that the Countess of Cassillis, in Ayrshire, ran away with the Gypsies and was pursued by the enraged Earl, who caught up with them and had Faa and his men hanged from the Dule tree of Cassillis, while his wife was forced to watch. Then he had her imprisoned in nearby Maybole Castle, with a window built into her wall facing the place of execution. Finally he had the faces of her lover and his companions carved into an outside staircase. It's a nice story, but the original ballad of Johnny Faa considerably pre-dates the period when the principals lived.

The last Queen of the Gypsies to live in the Palace at Kirk Yetholm was Esther Faa Blyth, who died in 1883, and it was not until 1898 that her son Charles Rutherford was persuaded to accept the position. He was crowned King Charles II on 30 May 1898. He died in 1902, bringing the tradition to an end. His widow lived on in the Palace until she died. Now, fully renovated, it is a self-catering cottage.

THE BASICS

Distance: 2½ miles / 4km

Gradient: Relatively flat. A gentle incline on the road back from point 4

Severity: Easy

Approx time to walk: 1½ hrs

Stiles: One (but it also has a gate beside it)

Map: OS Explorer OL16 (The Cheviot Hills)

Path description: Dirt footpaths, green tracks, country land and B road

Start point: Border Hotel, Kirk Yetholm, (GR NT827282)

Parking: By the village green (TD5 8PQ)

Landscape: Woodlands, pasture and village

Dog friendly: Dog-friendly walk, keep on leads near livestock

Public toilets: In Town Yetholm

Nearest food: Border Hotel, Kirk Yetholm. The village church does tea & coffee and biscuits every Wednesday from 10.30 to noon

KIRK YETHOLM WALK

1. From the Border Hotel walk back along the picturesque Main Street then take the first right turn. Continue along this lane to pass to the left of Kirk Yetholm Youth Hostel. Shortly after, pass to the left of a small bridge then, when the lane curves right towards Blunty's Mill, turn left onto the St Cuthbert's Way indicated by a way-marker.

2. Follow this narrow footpath through the woods until you reach a wooden gate. Go through it then veer left in the direction indicated by the way-marker. Cross the field, heading for a bridge, then go through another gate and up some steps onto the road. Cross over, then turn right. Pass an electrical substation to reach another way-marker, then turn left, go over a stile and into a field then head towards the pylon on the left. (There is a gate beside the stile.)

3. Veer right at the pylon, following the direction indicated by the way-marker, then follow the line of a fence. Continue following this narrow path, which gradually widens into a grassy track, to reach a gate. Go through this and continue following this track to reach a junction near the cemetery. Turn right and continue along the access road to reach the B6401.

4. Turn right and head along the road into Town Yetholm, keep straight along the High Street, then turn right into Dow Brae and follow it back to Kirk Yetholm and the start of the walk. Take some time to look at the memorial stone to the Gypsies in the square

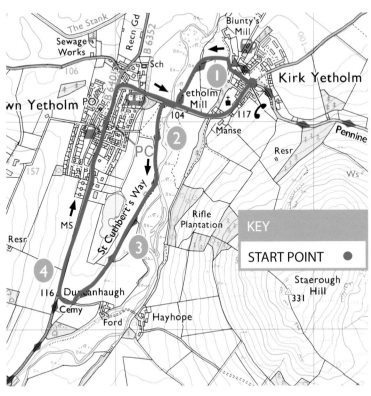

JEDBURGH ABBEY

This walk takes you through historic Jedburgh, by narrow alleyways and ancient buildings, including, possibly, the most beautiful Border abbey.

A priory of Augustinian Canons was established on this site by David I in 1118. By 1147 he had granted it abbey status. The massive building took centuries to complete and was an example of the very best of Norman and Early English architecture. The choir and nave were not added until the 13th century but were completed in time for the marriage of Alexander III to Yolande, daughter of the Compte de Dreux in 1285. Jedburgh was a powerful abbey with massive estates in Scotland and Northumberland and its abbot attended meetings of the Scottish Parliament. Like the other Border abbeys it was subject to attacks and invasions. In 1296 the abbot swore fealty to Edward I of England, but in 1297 the defeat of English forces by William Wallace at the Battle of Stirling Bridge resulted in an English revenge attack, when they wrecked and pillaged the abbey.

King Robert the Bruce continued to support the abbeys after Scottish Independence. In 1370 the Bruce's son, David II of Scotland, had the north transept completed but forty years later the attacks started again. They continued sporadically throughout the 15th century. Then in 1523 the Earl of Surrey set fire to the abbey and the

town and in 1544 the Earl of Hertford attacked. The resilient community of monks hung grimly on until 1560, when the Scottish Reformation finished it off. Even then the monks were allowed to remain, but the building became the parish kirk for the Protestant religion. This continued until 1871, when the building was considered too dangerous to continue using and a new church was built elsewhere.

The fortified house in Queen Street is where Mary Stuart, Queen of Scots stayed, when she visited the town in 1566. She became very ill while living there but when she heard that Lord Bothwell was lying wounded at Hermitage Castle near present-day Newcastleton, she rode there and back to see him. It was a round trip on horseback of forty miles across seriously difficult moorland and it took its toll on the young queen. The house is now a museum telling Mary's life story and has on display a death mask taken from her decapitated head after her execution at Fotheringhay Castle in Northamptonshire in 1587.

THE BASICS

Distance: 2 miles / 3km

Gradient: Some short and gentle inclines, and two sets of steps

Severity: Easy

Approx time to walk: ¾ hr to 1¼ hrs

Stiles: None

Map: OS Explorer OL16 (The Cheviot Hills)

Path description: Mainly pavement, with some rough tracks and footpaths

Start point: Car park at Abbey Bridge (GR NT 650202)

Parking: Abbey Bridge Car park (TD8 6JQ)

Landscape: Town streets, woodland and park

Dog friendly: This is a great walk for dogs

Public toilets: Next to café in the car park

Nearest food: Abbey Bridge Tollhouse Cafe

JEDBURGH ABBEY WALK

1. Exit the car park onto Abbey Place and turn left, heading along towards the abbey. Pass Abbey Bridge End, then the war memorial on your left, then cross the road to the Town Hall. Turn left in front of this and walk along a narrow lane between the Town Hall and the Carters Rest, passing a children's play area and a car park on your right, to reach Canongate.

2. Turn right then first left into Queen Street. Continue along this, ignoring the junction on your left, to reach Mary, Queen of Scots' House. Admission is free so why not spend some time visiting it?

3. Then turn left into Smith's Wynd and follow it to the junction with High Street and turn left. Walk along to return to Canongate, cross the road and head forwards towards the Bridewell Jail and the Sheriff Court House where Sir Walter Scott frequently appeared as an advocate in criminal trials.

4. Turn right then immediately left, at the end of the courthouse, into Castlegate. Cross the road and pass some narrow old closes: Cornelius Close, Nags Head Close and then Blackhills Close. A stone tablet on the front of the building tells you that Charles Edward Stuart (Bonnie Prince Charlie) lodged there overnight on 6–7 November 1745.

5. Re-cross the road and continue the long, gentle climb up Castlegate. When you reach Abbey Close turn right and go down it to the abbey. When you have finished looking at that come back up the close and continue your journey uphill. When you reach a set of steps climb up them onto Gala Hill, and then turn right to the Castle Jail and Museum. Again admission is free, so spend some time wandering round before returning to Gala Hill and turning right.

6. Head along, and then down Gala Hill, passing a cemetery on your right, then a House called Antylands. Shortly after this you will come to a way-marker pole on the left at the point where the road becomes a rough track. Turn left and go down some steps, then along a narrow path to reach a car parking area behind the bowling green. Keep straight ahead crossing this, then cross a bridge by another way-marker.

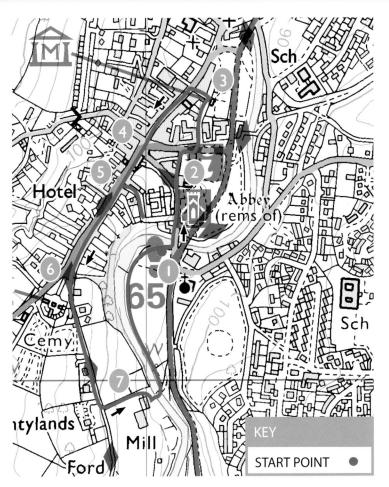

7. At the end of the bridge turn left at another way-marker and go down some steps to reach a footpath going through a small wooded area. This path emerges from the woods into Lothian Park. Continue following the path by the banks of the Jed Water to return to the car park.

JEDBURGH

Heritage trees are the theme of this walk, along with a small, fairy-tale castle and lush pastureland.

On this walk, you'll find an ancient, hollow oak with an enormous trunk some thirty feet (ten metres) in diameter. It's so old that the trunk has split and decayed and many of its heavy branches are propped up to prevent them breaking, but it is still alive and growing. It's one of the fifty most significant trees in the UK (one of only six in Scotland), selected by the National Tree Council to mark Queen Elizabeth's Golden Jubilee in 2002. The Capon Tree is about a thousand years old and is one of the last survivors from the ancient Jed Forest, which once covered most of the land in the Teviot Valley. There is a 19th-century painting of it by Arthur Perigal the younger, which you can see  in Jedburgh Castle Jail and Museum. You can see that it was a massive and ancient tree even then, with tiny people portrayed beside it.

There are several explanations of how it was named but it was probably because of the Capuchin monks, who sought shelter under its canopy as they travelled to and from Jedburgh Abbey. There was another Capon Tree near Brampton in Cumbria, on which six of Bonnie Prince Charlie's men were hanged in 1746. It died about a hundred years ago but a monument marks its location. The Jedburgh Capon Tree has also served on occasions as a hanging tree for public executions.

Another majestic old tree you will encounter on this walk is the King of the Woods. It's about twenty-three feet (seven metres) in girth and although not as old as the Capon Tree is still formidable.

Ferniehirst Castle is a lot younger than the two magnificent trees but still dates back to the late 15th century. It suffered greatly at the hands of invading English armies. Considerable damage was done to it from 1547 to 1549 during the 'Rough Wooing' (see Walk 4, Eyemouth) and indeed for much of the rest of the 16th century. Unused throughout the 18th century, it has undergone periodic restorations since 1830. It belonged to the Scottish Youth Hostels Association and functioned as a hostel until 1984. Then it was totally renovated and converted back to a private home by the 12th Marquess of Lothian. It is now used by his son, Lord Ralph Kerr and is occasionally open to the public.

THE BASICS

Distance: 4 miles / 6.5km

Gradient: A fairly undulating walk typical of the rolling hills of the Borders

Severity: Moderate

Approx time to walk: 2¼ hrs

Stiles: Four

Map: OS Explorer OL16 (The Cheviot Hills)

Path description: Footpaths, pastures, country lanes and roads

Start point: Car Park at Abbey Bridge (GR NT650202)

Parking: Abbey Bridge Car park (TD8 6JQ)

Landscape: Pastures, woodland and rolling hills

Dog friendly: Only if they can manage stiles

Public toilets: Next to café in the car park

Nearest food: Abbey Bridge Tollhouse Cafe

JEDBURGH WALK

1. From the car park take the riverside path heading away from the Abbey. Pass a way-marker and follow the path into woodlands, then climb some wooden steps and turn right onto a track. Follow this over a bridge, then cross a yard behind the bowling green and keep ahead on a narrow path. This heads uphill and onto a long set of steps.

2. At the top of the steps turn left onto the St Cuthbert's Way. This is a wide track heading downhill. Keep on it until a way-marker post just before a cottage, where you should veer left and head downhill on a narrow footpath. Head uphill again on more steps and then climb gently along a wide grassy path between two hedgerows.

3. When the path reaches Todlaw Farm keep ahead on the farm road in the direction indicated by the way-markers. When you reach a junction with a way-marker post at the end of the Todlaw Farm drive, turn left onto a country lane and keep on this until it reaches a T-junction with the A68.

4. Carefully cross the road here, turn right and continue along the pavement. Cross Hundalee Bridge, turn round a right-hand corner then cross the road to the Capon Tree, which is signposted. Don't go through the gate to get closer to the tree. It is 1,000 years old and parts of it are propped up. When you have seen the tree cross the road again and go across a stile into a field.

5. Head directly across this field to go over a stile by a gate and head uphill again through woodland. When you near the top you will find the King of the Forest on your right just before the gate. Cross a stile at the gate then veer right to head uphill across a grassy field towards the corner of a wood. When you reach the way-marker post turn right and walk along the edge of the wood, going through a gate with an electric fence on either side. Carefully unhook the coiled part of the fence by holding the insulated handle, go through, and then hook the fence up again. At the end of the second field cross a stile onto the access road to Ferniehirst Castle.

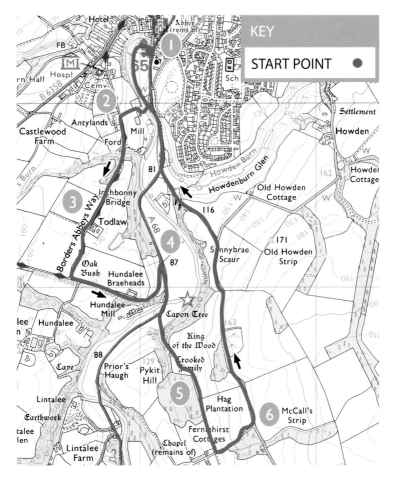

KEY

START POINT ●

6. It's a long, slow pull uphill from here. At the T-junction turn left towards Jedburgh and enjoy the walk along a very pleasant country lane. Eventually this will head downhill to reach a T-junction with the A68. Carefully cross this and turn right to head uphill on the pavement. Just over the hill you will see Jedburgh Abbey. Continue to reach the edge of the park, then turn left onto it and stroll across the grass to return to your car.

iStock

iStock

© Shutterstock / Patricia Hofmeester

MELROSE

THIS IS A PLEASANT WALK ALONG THE BANKS OF THE TWEED WITH ONE OF THE GREAT BORDER ABBEYS TO EXPLORE AT THE END.

Cistercian monks founded the Abbey of Melrose in 1136 at the request of David I of Scotland, and apparently had the east end completed within ten years. The rest of the building was completed during the next fifty years.

Like the other Border abbeys, Melrose was subject to many attacks. Edward II of England's army destroyed a large part of the building in 1322. It was subsequently rebuilt on the order of Robert the Bruce, whose heart was buried here in 1330. His body was interred at Dunfermline but his heart was taken on a Crusade to the Holy Land by his friend Sir James Douglas. Douglas was slain in battle in Moorish Grenada and the casket containing the heart was brought back to Melrose.

The abbey was destroyed again by fire in 1385, when the army of Richard II of England attacked. It took nearly a century to rebuild it. Then in 1544, during the Rough Wooing (see Walk 4, Eyemouth), English forces again caused extensive damage. It never really recovered after that attack. Further destruction was caused by cannon fire from Oliver Cromwell's forces during the English Civil War, but by then it was no longer a functioning monastery. The last abbot had died in 1559 and the sole surviving monk was dead by 1590. Part of the abbey's church became the parish kirk of Melrose for two centuries until 1810 when a new church was opened.

Just behind the town of Melrose are the Eildon Hills with their three summits and even more legends. In ancient tales they are said to be hollow, concealing within the Fairy Kingdom, where Thomas the Rhymer (see Walk 13, Newstead) was spirited away. Another tale tells of King Arthur and a host of armed knights with horses, asleep under the hills, while the legendary wizard, Michael Scot, who split the volcanic rock into three, features in James Hogg, the Ettrick Shepherd's 1823 novel, The Three Perils of Man, and in Walter Scott's Lay of the Last Minstrel. Whatever the truth of the legends, excavations show that people have occupied the hill over thousands of years. There was a massive Bronze Age hill fort here 3,000 years ago, while the Romans named the fort of Trimontium for this most significant landmark, which they used as a signal tower.

© Walter Baxter

© Richard West

THE BASICS

Distance: 3½ miles / 5.5km

Gradient: Mainly flat walk with a few easy inclines

Severity: Easy

Approx time to walk: 2 hrs

Stiles: None

Map: OS Explorer 338 (Galashiels, Selkirk and Melrose)

Path description: Pavement, surfaced roads and footpaths

Start point: Car park opposite Melrose Abbey (GR NT547341)

Parking: Car park at abbey (TD6 9LG)

Dog friendly: An excellent dog walk

Public toilets: Near the end of the walk beside Melrose Rugby Club

Nearest food: Abbey Coffee Shop beside the car park or the Abbey Mill Tea Room

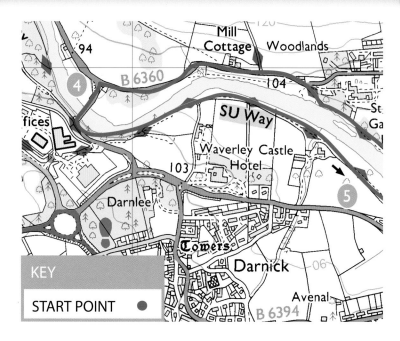

KEY

START POINT ●

1. Exit the car park and cross to the abbey. Turn left and go along the street, passing a road junction at Harmony Gardens and keeping ahead by the sign for Newstead and Edinburgh. This is St Mary's Road. Pass the Abbey Mill, which has a splendid tea room. When the road bends right, turn left onto Chain Bridge Road. This is also signposted for the Border Abbeys Way.

2. Enjoy this pretty country lane on the edge of town and the view as you approach the Chain Link Bridge. It was built in 1826 and was originally a toll bridge. The building at its southern end is the old toll house. Cross the bridge then turn left onto the Southern Upland Way (SUW).

3. Keep to the SUW along the riverside path with woodland to your left for the next three-quarters of a mile (1km). You'll see aspen, willow and alder all growing here. Also see if you can spot wild birds like goosander, mallard and the odd heron. Follow the path for a few hundred yards and then head uphill through the woods to pass to the left of a cottage and reach the B6360. Turn left here and continue along a pavement to reach a T-junction with the B6374.

4. Turn left towards Melrose on the B6374. Continue on this road then cross the bridge over the Tweed. This is the Lowood Bridge but is also known as the Bottle Brig because a bottle was built into the structure. Follow the road round to the left

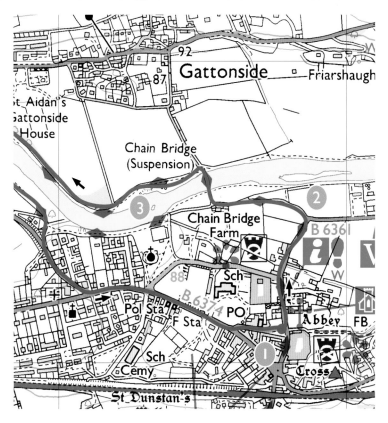

after the bridge and continue along a pavement on the left-hand side of the road. This is part of the Border Abbeys Way. Opposite the next road junction on your right is a set of finger posts. Turn left here and continue along the Border Abbeys Way/Southern Upland Way. Go through a gate and continue on a well-surfaced footpath, which passes 'Skirmish Field', the site of a battle which took place in 1526 between prominent Border families and the supporters of King James V. The path now heads downhill to go along the riverbank.

5. Eventually this will turn right to go through a kissing gate onto Waverley Road. Keep left, ignoring the SUW way-marker pointing left, and keep ahead, passing Tweed Cottage, to climb a set of steps onto Waverley Road. Turn left and continue along, crossing over the junction with St Mary's Road then pass Melrose Rugby Football ground and the public toilets. When the road forks, turn left along Buccleuch Street to return to the car park.

NEWSTEAD ROMAN FORT

WALK THROUGH BORDERS HISTORY FROM THE ROMAN FORT AT TRIMONTIUM TO THE MEDIAEVAL BARD, THOMAS THE RHYMER AND FINALLY TO A MAGNIFICENT VICTORIAN RAILWAY VIADUCT.

The walk starts at the stone of Thomas the Rhymer, who was a real historical character by the name of Thomas of Erceldoune. He wrote poems and made prophesies and was much respected in the late 13th century. He is believed to have written *Sir Tristrem*, later edited by Walter Scott and thought to be the oldest known piece of Scots poetry. Although Thomas was a real person, you can make up your own mind about the story of the stone.

Legend has it that while out walking in the Eildon Hills, Thomas fell asleep for what seemed to him like a few minutes but was in fact years. During this time, he was spirited away by the Queen of the Fairies. When she returned him to the mortal world she gave him the gift of prophecy. Thomas used his powers to predict several significant events in Scotland's history, which included the death of King Alexander III in 1296, the succession of Robert the Bruce to the throne, the Scots' defeat at Flodden in 1513 and the Union of the Crowns in 1603. His story is told in the ballad of 'Thomas the Rhymer' in Sir Walter Scott's collection *Minstrelsy of the Scottish Border*.

As you walk on, you find yourself moving deeper into Borders history. The Borders of the past was a turbulent place, far removed from the peaceful land you see today. The Romans failed to hold very much of Scotland but they fought for a hundred years over this area. There is not much to see on the ground, but the information boards bring it to life. Don't miss stopping to read and to look, to help you imagine this bustling settlement as it would have been. It is still possible to make out the unmistakable shape of the amphitheatre.

Behind the amphitheatre as you turn towards the start of the walk, the 19th century looms. The elegant Leaderfoot Viaduct was admired by Queen Victoria, who described it as 'immense'. It was opened in October 1865 to carry the Berwickshire Railway, from Reston on the East Coast Main Line to St Boswells on the Waverley Line. The 19 arches – each with a 43-foot (13m) span – are of brickwork while the abutments, piers and walls are rustic-faced red sandstone.

THE BASICS

Distance: 2 miles / 3km
Gradient: Mainly flat
Severity: Easy
Approx time to walk: 1½ hrs
Stiles: One
Map: OS Explorer 338 (Galashiels, Selkirk and Melrose)
Path description: Country lanes, farmland, old railway tracks & footpaths
Start point: Information Board on Thomas the Rhymer, on minor road off A6091 south-east of Melrose (GR NT564335)
Parking: Lay-by next to the information board on Thomas the Rhymer (TD6 9HA)
Landscape: Fields, hills and river
Dog Friendly: Dog friendly apart from the stile
Public toilets: Melrose, Abbey Street
Nearest food: Melrose

1. From the parking walk on to the information board on Thomas the Rhymer. Continue on the road from here through a gate and on to the Rhymer's Stone. This is the site of the Eildon Tree, where Thomas was supposed to have met the Fairy Queen. Go along the path to the left from the stone to the viewpoint, from which on a clear day you can see the Leaderfoot Bridges over the Tweed. Between the stone and the viewpoint there is a well-made stony path running between two hedges; follow this long, straight path to a farm track.

2. Turn right down the farm track to a busy road. Cross to another farm track leading to Broomhill Farm. Follow this track uphill past some farm sheds and immediately look for a narrow path going off to the left into the bushes. This leads on to the disused railway track.

3. The track goes under a bridge and continues to an information board about Trimontium, the first of several. Just beyond the board there is a viewing platform, which gives a better view of the site. Return to the information board and cross the stile and turn right along the edge of the field.

4. When you reach the road, go through the gate and turn left after stopping to admire the magnificent Leaderfoot Viaduct to your right. Continue along the road to Newsteads, stopping at the interpretation boards on the way to find out where the various parts of the fort would have been. When you reach the main road turn right through Newsteads.

5. Near the end of the village you will see Claymires Lane on the left. Turn up here and at the top go right and then left under the old railway bridge and the subway under the road. Turn left towards two gates. Go through the gate on the left to follow the Eildon Hills Path back to the old road and then turn left to return to the start of the walk

THE BATTLE OF PHILIPHAUGH

WALK AROUND THE SITE OF A 17TH-CENTURY BATTLE
BETWEEN ROYALISTS AND COVENANTERS, WHERE
INFORMATION BOARDS ON SITE BRING THE PAST TO LIFE.

On 13 September 1645, Philiphaugh, south-west of Selkirk, was the site of an important battle between the Royalists and the Parliamentarians. The Covenanters were supporters of a Scottish Presbyterian faith, upon which the king was forcing change. So in defence of their faith they allied themselves with the Parliamentarians. The Royalists were supporters of Charles I. The Marquis of Montrose, the leader of the Royalist Army, had been routing the Covenanters across Scotland in a series of battles. His opponent, General Sir David Leslie, leader of the Covenanters, was a seasoned commander with thirty years' experience.

Montrose marched to Selkirk on 12 September 1645, with 1,000 foot soldiers and 500 cavalry, hoping to recruit more soldiers to the Royalist cause. But the lowlands of Scotland, where Covenanters in their hundreds were attending secret outdoor services in remote glens, and ministers were being hanged, shot or imprisoned by the king's soldiers, was not fertile recruiting territory for the Crown.

In fact Leslie was given information about every move Montrose made. Montrose and his officers spent the night in Selkirk town while his troops camped in the fields at Philiphaugh. Leslie, who had 4,000 foot soldiers and 2,000 cavalry, made a surprise attack in the early morning mist of 13 September. Montrose rallied his troops against a second attack but meanwhile Leslie had sent 2,000 horsemen around Howden Hill to attack the Royalist army from the rear.

With Leslie attacking from the front and the cavalry behind, the Royalists panicked and the cavalry fled, leaving the foot soldiers surrounded. They were promised their freedom if they surrendered, but in fact they were massacred without pity. Some managed to escape, some were killed on the battlefield and the rest, including women, were taken as prisoners to Newark Castle, where they were shot and buried at a spot now known as Slain Men's Lea (see Walk 15, Bowhill).

Montrose fled across the Minch Moor towards Traquair and later, having been defeated at Carisdale in 1650, he was captured, tried and executed in Edinburgh. His severed head was displayed on a spike above the Tolbooth. Leslie was awarded a substantial amount of money for his service at Philiphaugh. After Charles II had accepted the Covenant, Leslie joined the Royalist army and was eventually ennobled as Lord Newark by Charles II. Leslie died in 1682.

THE BASICS

Distance: 2 miles / 3km

Gradient: Flat level going

Severity: Easy

Approx time to walk: 1 hr

Stiles: None

Map: OS Explorer 338 (Galashiels, Selkirk and Melrose)

Path description: Grassy paths and pavements

Start point: Car Park, Philipshaugh (GR NT4502727787)

Parking: Car park (TD7 5LU)

Dog friendly: On leads for preference

Public toilets: Selkirk: Dovecot, Scotts Place, TD7 4DP

Nearest food: Waterwheel Tearoom in car park

1. Before you set out on this walk, have a good look at the information board in the car park, which gives all the details of the battle including maps. Then cross behind the tearoom to a path alongside the road. Continue on this path, stopping to read the very informative interpretation boards as you go.

2. Eventually you will reach a memorial stone to those who fell in the battle. Continue from here to turn right alongside a fence and emerge in a field. Bear left, walking along the edge of the field to a gate onto the A708.

3. Go through the gate and turn right. Follow the road to a T-junction and turn right onto the A707. At the next junction, just before the bridge turn right into Ettrickhaugh Road, passing the rugby ground on the right.

4. At the end of the row of houses on the left turn left to cross a bridge and follow the red way-markers along a path, eventually passing the fish farm to your right. Look out for the ducks and hens here. Continue to follow the path around some buildings to reach the long, straight stretch of the mill lade.

5. Continue along the mill lade until the path forks away from it to the left. Follow this path until you come to a right turn over a bridge to the old mill and salmon viewing centre. Take this road back to the car park.

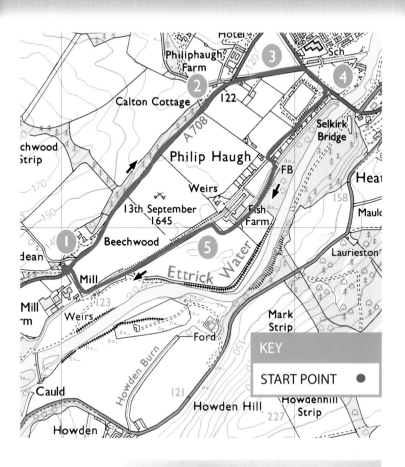

BOWHILL – THE LADY'S WALK

A LOVELY WOODLAND WALK TO A RUINED AND
ATMOSPHERIC TOWER, WHICH WAS A ROYAL HUNTING
LODGE AND THE SITE OF MURDER MOST FOUL.

Newark Tower, just west of Selkirk, is a 15th-century stone keep and courtyard fortress, founded by Archibald, Earl of Douglas around 1423. Douglas called it the 'New Werk' to distinguish it from the nearby 'Auldwark', of which there is now no trace. The building was completed by about 1475 and the battlements and caphouses were added about 1600. Sitting on a knoll above the Yarrow Water, it is a traditional five-storey tower with two 16th-century, two-storey caphouses on opposing angles. In 1455, the castle came to the Crown and in 1473 King James III gave it to his wife, Margaret of Denmark as the royal hunting lodge for Ettrick Forest. The royal arms can be seen on the west gable.

Newark withstood a siege by the English army in 1547, but was burnt and taken by them the following year. In 1645, after the Battle of Philiphaugh (see Walk 14), 100 Royalist followers, mainly Irish, were shot in the courtyard and buried on Slain Men's Lea. Some say the castle is haunted by the souls of the murdered women and children, who are heard lamenting each year on 13 September. After the Battle of Dunbar in 1650 it fell to Cromwell's invading army.

By the end of the 17th century it belonged to the Scotts of Buccleuch, who still own it, and was altered for Anne Scott, the 1st Duchess of Buccleuch. She lived there as a widow after her husband, James, the Duke of Monmouth was executed for rising up against the Crown. Sir Walter Scott mentions it in the *The Lay of the Last Minstrel*...

He passed where Newark's stately tower
Looks out from Yarrow's birchen bower:
The Minstrel gazed with wishful eye –
No humbler resting-place was nigh.

…

The Duchess marked his weary pace,
His timid mien and reverend face.

…

For she had known adversity,
Though born in such a high degree;
In pride of power, in beauty's bloom,
Had wept over Monmouth's bloody tomb!

Unless you happen to be visiting on a Tuesday, make time before or after your walk to explore Bowhill, the beautiful Georgian house which is home to the Duchess's descendants. Or take the children to the adventure playground and see the priceless art treasures another day.

THE BASICS

Distance: 3 miles / 5km
Gradient: Some short inclines but mainly flat level going
Severity: Easy
Approx time to walk: 1 to 1½ hrs
Stiles: None
Map: OS Explorer 338 (Galashiels, Selkirk and Melrose)
Path description: Estate roads and paths
Start point: Car park at Bowhill (GR NT425278)
Parking: Car park (TD7 5ET)
Landscape: Pastureland and woodland
Dog friendly: Good dog walk but keep on leads near livestock
Public toilets: At Bowhill
Nearest food: Café at Bowhill, but closed Tuesdays except July and August

BOWHILL – THE LADY'S WALK

1. Exit the car park and turn right onto an estate road in the direction indicated by the finger post for the Lady's Walk. Head downhill, then turn left to walk in front of the arched entrance to some of the estate buildings. At a junction, keep ahead following the red way-markers. Pass a children's' adventure playground and keep ahead at the next crossroads, then keep left where the road forks.

2. This is the Lime Avenue, a leafy lane lined with lime trees. When you reach the next fork, keep left again then turn immediately right onto a footpath as indicated by a red way-marker. Follow this downhill through woodland, and when it forks again keep right. The path follows the river and you'll come across a bench where you can enjoy a grand view of the water. Then continue, head uphill and up some steps to reach another well-placed bench at a junction of paths at the top. Turn right and continue following the path by the river.

3. Cross an old stone bridge over the Newark Burn and then pass to the left of a more modern, metal one round about the one-mile (1.5km) mark. The path now has trees and the river to the right, and open fields on the left side with views over the estate. When you see a cottage in front and to the left of you look uphill to the left for your first view of Newark Castle.

4. The path ends at a T-junction by Newarkmill. Turn left and follow the estate road as it curves to the left and uphill. When you reach a gate, go through it, turn right and continue up the estate road to visit Newark Castle.

5. Then return to the gate and go to the left of Newark Cottage. At a junction go left and follow this road, to pass by The Old Schoolhouse. This is the part known as Slain Men's' Lea, where the murdered prisoners from the Battle of Philiphaugh were buried (see Walk 14, the Battle of Philiphaugh).

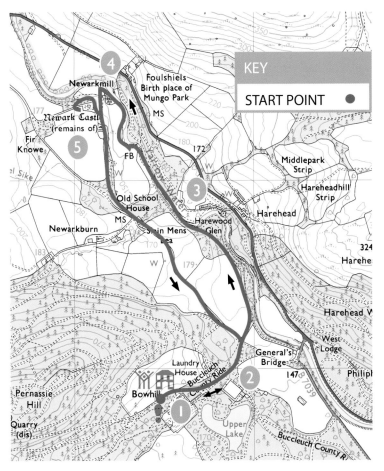

KEY

START POINT ●

6. Eventually reach the junction with the Lime Avenue and retrace the earlier part of your route to return to the car park.

CARDRONA FOREST

THIS IS A FOREST WALK BY A RIVER WHERE YOU CAN
IDENTIFY MANY NATIVE SPECIES OF TREE.

This delightful walk is perfect for children to get to know our native trees and the conifers that have been introduced for commercial timber production. Take along a book of trees for more detailed identification. The first part of the walk, alongside a bubbling tree-lined river, is where you will find deciduous trees.

Alder usually grows on riverbanks. In summer look for the rounded leaves, tapering towards the stalk, with a toothed edge. In spring and early summer look for the flowers, dark yellow/brown male catkins and smaller red, cone-shaped female flowers. In autumn these turn into small green cones, which become woody in winter.

In spring the ash produces small, green flowers before the leaves. In summer the leaves have a central stem with leaflets in pairs, with one at the tip. By autumn the flowers have become ash keys, hanging in clusters. In winter look for the distinctive grey bark and black buds.

The mountain ash or rowan has leaves similar to the ash but smaller. In summer look for clusters of white flowers, which in autumn become orange or red berries.

The silver birch is readily identified by its tall, slender, silver-barked trunk. The leaves are small and almost triangular with a serrated edge. In spring look for the female and male flowers, while later you can see the female catkins hanging.

Hawthorn can be either a bush or a small tree. The small, lobed leaves appear early. By late spring and early summer it is covered with a profusion of small, white flowers, known as 'May Blossom', from which comes the saying, 'Ne'er cast a cloot till May is oot.' In the autumn, the flowers become dark red berries.

The return part of the walk is through the dappled green canopy of the conifer forest.

The Sitka spruce, introduced in the 19th century, is cone-shaped with long branches hanging down from the pointed top. The needles are greenish blue and very sharp. The larch, introduced in the 17th century, is deciduous. So in spring its leaves are a fresh green among the dark conifers, in autumn it glows golden, while in winter its brown, leafless shape stands out. The Scots Pine, which is the only native conifer, has a distinctive shape, with a long trunk spreading at the top into a broad canopy.

THE BASICS

Distance: 2½ miles / 4km
Gradient: Slow easy uphill, then downhill return
Severity: Easy
Approx time to walk: 1¼ hrs
Stiles: None
Map: OS Explorer 337 (Peebles and Innerleithen)
Path description: Forestry roads and paths
Start point: Forestry Commission car park (GR NT 293384)
Parking: At start (EH45 9HU)
Landscape: Forest and river side
Dog friendly: An excellent walk for dogs
Public toilets: At car park
Nearest food: Peebles

CARDRONA FOREST WALK

1. From the car park head to the right of the toilet block and follow the white, blue and red way-markers. You can do this walk either way round, but following these directions means it's a gentler climb up the side of Pikes Knowe.

2. Where the paths divide, at a footbridge, keep ahead on a forest road. Follow this as it climbs steadily uphill with the Kirk Burn to your right.

3. When you reach some woodland on the right with the buildings of Laverlaw above you to the right you are about halfway to the top.

4. When you come to a junction in the road, keep left, following Glenpeggy Burn Road. The one to the right is Kirk Burn Road. The ascent gets a bit steeper here as the road turns to the left. Pass one way-marker pole, then shortly after come to a second with the number 4 on it.

5. Turn left here following blue and red way-marker poles uphill on a footpath through the woods. This can be rather muddy in sections. Shortly you will come to another way-marker and to the right of it a narrower footpath heads steeply uphill. This is the path to Castle Knowe, and you can climb up there for the views then return to this spot. Alternatively you can continue from there following the red way-markers to pass the remains of the Cardrona Tower.

6. Otherwise keep ahead, climbing steadily. Eventually the path reaches the top of the hill and continues down the other side. Keep on it until you reach a blue and red way-marker pole indicating a left turn down a narrower path through the trees.

7. Keep on this downhill to arrive at a ford with a bridge beside it. Turn left over the bridge then right onto the forest road and return to the start.

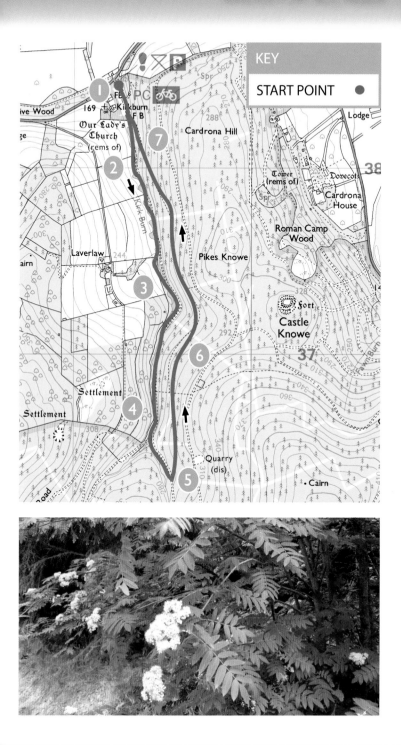

PEEBLES TOWN

PEEBLES IS ONE OF THE PRETTIEST AND MOST INTERESTING BORDERS TOWNS WITH EVIDENCE OF THE TOWN'S PAST AT EVERY STEP.

The traditional Mercat Cross in the High Street has stood in a number of different spots, which would once have marked the commercial centre of the town where people gathered for trade and meetings and news.

The Chambers Institute was the town residence in Peebles of the noble family of March and of the Duke of Queensberry, after whom it came to be known as the Queensberry Lodging. On a town plan of 1775, it was called Dean's House, and opposite you can see Dean's Wynd, which led from the Dean's House to the Cross Kirk. It was bought by William Chambers, the founder of W & R Chambers, publishers, in 1857 and completely remodelled by 1859, for use as a library, art gallery and museum. The wall thicknesses, part-vaulted basement

and a window lintel bearing the date '1668' testify to its 16th or 17th-century origins. Don't miss the unusual mosaic war memorial unveiled by Earl Haig in 1922.

A little further along the High Street take a closer look at the two historic inns, the County Inn and the Tontine Hotel. The 18th-century facade of the County conceals an older 'bastel house' with thick barrel-vaulted walls. The elegant Georgian Tontine Hotel, like many so-named inns of the time, was built in 1808 on the tontine principle, by a number of investors, of whom the last surviving inherited the whole.

The Tweed Bridge is an ancient river crossing, first built in stone in 1485, replacing a former wooden bridge. Look under the bridge to see the original 15th-century bridge, just wide enough for a horse and cart, still clearly visible, as is the widening of 1834 and of 1900.

Parliament Square, just off the High Street, was so called because the Scottish Parliament supposedly met here in 1346. Whether that is true or not, there is an interesting marriage lintel, carved with 'RS:HM 1743' and a mason's square and compasses, and the 'Stinking Stair', which led down to the brewery and tannery on Tweed Green.

There is much more to discover but one of the delights of a visit to Peebles, as with many Border towns, is the almost total absence of chain stores. Instead there are many small, quirky craft shops, particularly around the High Street and School Brae.

THE BASICS

Distance: 2 miles / 3km

Gradient: Negligible

Severity: Easy

Approx time to walk: 1½ hrs

Stiles: None

Map: OS Landranger 73 (Peebles, Galashiels & Selkirk) (Or pick up Town Map from the TIC)

Path description: Pavements, paths and cobbled streets

Start point: The Cross Kirk to the north of the town centre (GR NT249407)

Parking: Next to the Cross Kirk (EH45 8LE)

Landscape: Historic buildings and riverside

Nearest refreshment: There are many cafés and pubs around the High Street

PEEBLES TOWN WALK

1. From the car park go and have a look at the ruined Cross Kirk. From here turn right into Cross Road and then along St Andrew's Road to the town cemetery and St Andrew's Tower, which is all that remains of the 13th-century St Andrew's Church. Cross the road from here into Hay Lodge Park, where there is a children's play park. Follow the riverside path back towards the town, passing the swimming pool and arriving at the Tweed Bridge.

2. Turn right and cross the bridge and then turn left into King's Meadow and continue along the riverside path to cross the ornate white iron footbridge to Tweed Green or the Washing Green, where the people used to dry their laundry and still have the right to do so. Walk along Tweed Green as far as School Brae.

3. At the foot of School Brae, you can see two old schools: on the left with three fishes carved on the pediment is the English School, dating from 1766; and on the right is the Grammar School, built in 1812; look here for a carved St Andrew's cross and a carved G. Further along to the right is the Cabbage Hall, which was the schoolmaster's house. As you go up School Brae, you can see on your left the Burgh School, built in 1886, now converted into craft workshops. Go through the arch at the top of School Brae into the High Street. Immediately opposite is a former bakery; look for the stone panel on the wall.

4. Turn left along the High Street passing, to your left, the Old Town House, the County Hotel and the Tontine Hotel and, on the right, Scott Brothers' ironmongery, a house with a sundial and the old cinema. When you reach a cobbled bend on the left go down it to Parliament Square, continue down the 'Stinking Stair' to the Tweed Green and turn right to come up the Port Brae and turn right back into the High Street.

5. At the end of the High Street are the magnificent Peebles Old Parish Church and the Sheriff Court House. Turning back along the High Street Messrs Whitie's newsagents is on the right and, opposite, the Bank House. Retrace your steps past School Brae and look for the imposing Chambers Institution with two ornate lamp standards outside. Go through to the quadrangle to see the war memorial. From here go on past the Mercat Cross to Venland Road on the left to see the only surviving piece of the old 16th-century town wall.

6. Return to the Mercat Cross and turn into Northgate. On the right is the Cross Keys Inn. Look for the Northgate Garden, where you can see the four pedestal tablets of the Mercat Cross. Also look out for the marriage lintels on some of the older houses, with the date when the house was built and the initials of the couple

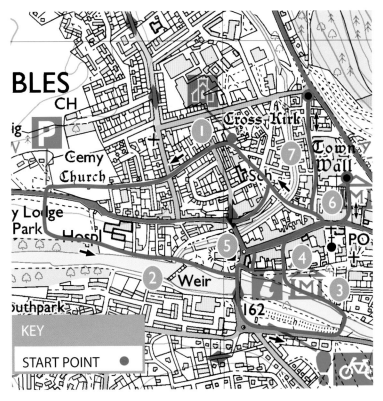

who lived there. Return to the Masonic Hall on the corner and turn right into Bridgegate.

7. Continue to cross the bridge over Eddleston Water. On the left here is a house with a lion carved above the door; this was formerly the Red Lion Inn. From here turn left into Biggiesknowe, where the older houses are weavers' cottages, built in 1796. William and Robert Chambers the publishers were born in one of these cottages in 1800 and 1802. Retrace your steps as far as Old Church Road and go along here to return to the Cross Kirk.

© Shutterstock / Victor Denovan

NEIDPATH CASTLE

STROLL ALONG THE BANKS OF THE RIVER TWEED TO NEIDPATH CASTLE, CROSS THE NEIDPATH VIADUCT ON THE OLD CALEDONIA RAILWAY LINE, THEN RETURN TO PEEBLES ON THE OPPOSITE BANK.

This walk along the banks of a famous Scottish salmon river and through woodland has lots of interesting things to see. Take a couple of pocket field guides for trees and wild flowers and see how many you, or the children, can identify. Once you get the first glimpse of Neidpath Castle through the leaves it's time for a ghost story. Walter Scott tells it beautifully in his poem 'The Maid of Neidpath'.

It's a classic tale of a forbidden love between two young people. Jean Douglas, youngest daughter of the Earl of March, fell for the son of the Laird of Tushielaw. His lower social station meant that he was not considered a suitable match and so Lord March had him banished to fight abroad. Lady Jean was distraught and went into decline, rapidly losing weight. By the time young Tushielaw returned from abroad she was so emaciated that he rode past without recognising her. As in all tragic love stories she died shortly thereafter and, ever since, her ghost, clad in a long brown dress with a white collar, flits through the castle on occasion.

In the late 20th century the Dumfriesshire songwriter and musician Lionel McClelland took the story and wrote his song 'The Earl o' March's Daughter', bringing the story to the attention of an entirely new audience.

Neidpath Castle was originally built by Gilbert Fraser, around the end of the 12th century, and then replaced sometime in the late 14th century by Sir William Hay after his family had acquired it by marriage. As a defensive building it saw its share of warfare, particularly during Oliver Cromwell's invasion in 1650 when it was damaged by artillery fire. Eventually it passed into the ownership of William Douglas, who was later created

the Earl of March. It is his daughter who allegedly haunts the building. But before you rush uphill on a ghost hunt, bear in mind that Neidpath is not open to the public other than for organised and pre-arranged group tours.

The next thing you will encounter on this walk is the eight stone skew arches of Neidpath Viaduct. That's the midpoint of the walk, where you cross the river and start back down the other side.

THE BASICS

Distance: 3 miles / 5km

Gradient: Mostly level with a little undulation

Severity: Easy but with a short section from the viaduct back down to the riverbank where the path is narrow and greater care is needed

Approx time to walk: 1½ to 2 hours

Stiles: None

Map: OS Explorer 337 (Peebles and Innerleithen)

Path description: Paved footpath, dirt footpath and old railway trackbed

Start point: Car park at Peebles Swimming Pool (GR NT249403)

Parking: Car park (EH45 8AW)

Landscape: Riverside, woodland and park

Dog friendly: Yes

Public toilets: On south side of park, close to café and bowling greens

Nearest food: Many cafés, pubs and restaurants in Peebles

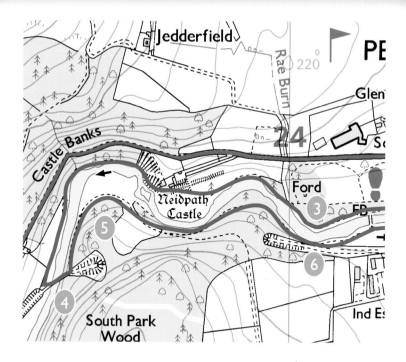

1. From the car park head past the swimming pool and turn right onto a well-paved path running beside the river. Cross a metal footbridge and continue past some benches onto a dirt path. When the path ends at some stone steps, head up them, then turn left through an opening and along the back of a large white building before descending by a similar set of steps to rejoin the riverside path.

2. The path enters Hay Park, passing a metal Victorian Bridge on the left and a children's play park on the right. At the end of the park a finger post points to the Tweed Walk, Neidpath Castle and Lyne Station. Follow the path in the direction of the arrow.

3. Take care when you cross a low, narrow bridge and continue on a rough footpath. This can be smooth and rocky and with exposed tree roots. Occasionally it will climb over a hillock or two. Cross another bridge, go through a gate and shortly Neidpath Castle will be visible through the trees. The path winds past the castle and continues to go through a kissing gate.

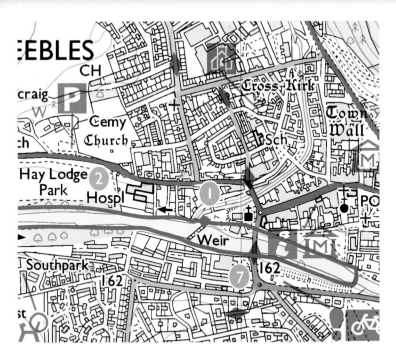

4. Eventually you will see Neidpath Viaduct spanning the river in front of you. When you reach it, turn right and head up a series of steps to reach the old trackbed on top of the viaduct. A finger post points the way to Lyne Station. But turn left here and head along the old railway line on the River Tweed Walk. The viaduct is also known as The Queens Bridge and it was built in 1863 to carry the Symington to Peebles branch of the Caledonian Railway. It has been closed since 1954 but is still in use as a footpath. It's a Category A listed structure and one of the finest examples of skew arch construction in the country.

5. At the end of the viaduct you will see the Neidpath Tunnel up ahead. Tempting as it is, this is not the route to follow. Instead turn left and head downhill on a rough, narrow and uneven path. This will soon reach the riverbank and you will have even better views of Neidpath Castle. The path then goes through woodland before emerging into Hay Park.

6. Continue on the footpath past the Victorian Bridge and follow the path with a grand view of the town before you, to reach the main bridge over the Tweed in Peebles. A rough path heads down to the water's edge and there is a way under the bridge and out onto the path at the other side, but avoid this with young children and when the river is in spate. Instead head up some steps onto the bridge, carefully cross the road and go down the steps on the other side.

7. From here continue to reach another metal bridge. Cross this and then turn left to continue down the path on the opposite bank. The good people of Peebles have the right to dry their washing on this green and you will see the clothes poles installed for that purpose. Eventually cross under the bridge again and return to the swimming pool and the start of the walk.

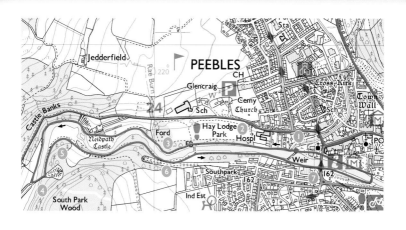

BROUGHTON

THIS IS A LANDSCAPE THAT THE SECRET SERVICE AGENT
RICHARD HANNAY WOULD HAVE LOVED. IT'S A LOT LIKE
SOME OF THE COUNTRYSIDE HE WOULD HAVE TRAVELLED
THROUGH IN JOHN BUCHAN'S MOST FAMOUS NOVEL, *THE
THIRTY-NINE STEPS*.

Buchan is primarily remembered as the writer of the first spy novel. Hannay, his main character, was apparently created during a period when Buchan was convalescing. 'I invented a young South African called Richard Hannay … and I amused myself with considering what he would do in various emergencies.' Hannay was allegedly modelled on the Edinburgh-born Edmund Ironside, a friend of Buchan from his days spent in Africa. Ironside had briefly been a bona fide spy. But Buchan was much more than a novelist. The bulk of his output was non-fiction, including biographies and histories.

Born the son of a minister in Perth in 1875, he was brought up in Fife but spent the long summer holidays exploring the countryside around Broughton while staying with his maternal grandparents. Later he would use local place names for characters in his novels. His character Sir Edward Leithen was named after Leithen Water, a tributary of the Tweed. After university he became a career diplomat and secretary to the High Commissioner for Southern Africa. Extensive travel there provided him with lots more material for his books – as well as inspiration for Richard Hannay.

Later he became editor of *The Spectator* and qualified as a barrister, although he never actually practised law. But he and his brother Walter founded a firm of solicitors, J. & W Buchan, which exists to this day in Peebles.

During the First World War he was in France working as a correspondent for *The Times* as well as continuing to write fiction. *The Thirty-Nine Steps*, which dealt with the period just before the outbreak of war, was published in 1915. Twenty years later it became a film, directed by Alfred Hitchcock and starring Robert Donat as Hannay.

Eventually Buchan enlisted in the army and was posted to the Intelligence Corps, and he was eventually appointed as Director of Information. After the war he continued writing as well as becoming actively involved in politics. In 1935 he was created Baron Tweedsmuir of Elsfield and shortly afterwards appointed Governor General of Canada. He died in Canada in 1940 following a stroke.

Although most of his adult life was spent outside of Scotland he retained a deep affection for it, particularly this part of the Borders.

THE BASICS

Distance: 4½miles / 7.25 km
Gradient: Some gentle inclines, otherwise flat level going
Severity: Easy
Approx time to walk: 2½ to 3 hrs
Stiles: None
Map: OS Explorer 336 (Biggar and Broughton)
Path description: Gravel tracks, paved roads and dirt footpaths
Start point: Shepherds Cottage, Broughton Place, Broughton (GR NT119375)
Parking: Car Park at start (free) (ML12 6HJ)
Landscape: Hills, pastures, old railways and roads
Dog friendly: Much of the route crosses livestock areas, so please follow the Scottish Outdoor Access Code. During the lambing period (March to May) please avoid taking dogs.
Public toilets: In the car park in front of Broughton Primary School
Nearest food: Laurel Bank Tea Room in the centre of Broughton

BROUGHTON WALK

1. From the car park head back along the track, then onto a metalled lane past Broughton Place, through stone gate posts and twisting round the steading of Broughton Place Farm to eventually reach a T-junction with the A701. Turn left onto it and proceed through the village, passing Laurel Bank Tea Room on your right, then turn left into Dreva Road and past Springwell Brae.

2. After this leaves the village it becomes a rather pretty country lane that eventually starts to climb up the side of Dreva Hill. Slow down and take this section easy. And stop often to admire the views over to your right. Eventually you will start down the other side of the hill and below you to the right you will see the line of the old railways. When you reach a junction, at a hairpin bend, turn right towards Rachan and continue downhill.

3. Keep on this lane until it turns left to go under a railway bridge. On the other side turn right and take a path that leads up the banking and onto the old trackbed. Turn left.

4. At first this is a well-surfaced track going through a gate, passing a cellphone mast and going through another gate to cross a bridge over Biggar Water. When the track veers left, to end at a gate by a field, keep ahead on a narrow footpath and keep on it until it reaches a footbridge crossing the water to your right. The path ahead reaches a gate, but before you reach it turn left and follow a path to another gate. Go through this and continue on a well-trodden grassy path through a field to exit onto the A701 via a gate. In front of you is the Broughton, Glenholm and Kilbucho church.

5. Turn right and walk along the A701, entering Broughton village, and passing the village school and war memorial. Eventually at the end of the village turn right onto the John Buchan Way and return to the car park.

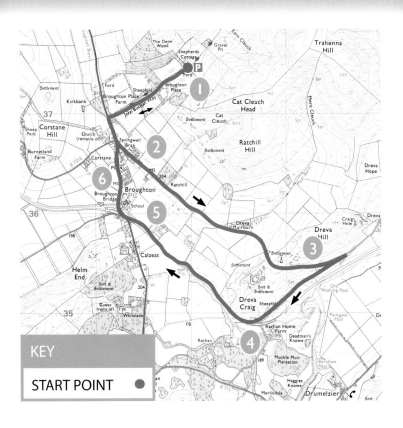

KEY

START POINT ●

NEWCASTLETON

AN 18TH-CENTURY PLANNED VILLAGE, A FORGOTTEN
RAILWAY LINE, THE CEMETERY FROM A VANISHED
SETTLEMENT AND A 14TH-CENTURY STONE CROSS MAKE
THIS A VERY INTERESTING WALK.

This delightful Borders village was created, in 1793, by the 3rd Duke of Buccleuch after he had cleared his tenants from the settlement of Old Castleton. His plan was to create a centre developing flax, wool and cotton, which would then be turned into cloth by his tenants, the handloom weavers.

Newcastleton was built on the site of an old tower called Copshaw and to this day villagers still call it Copshaw Holm or Copshaw. If you visit on the weekend of the long-running folk festival (first weekend in July) you may hear the traditional song 'Copshawholm Fair' that was written back in 1830 and for many years was sung by the famous Border Shepherd Willie Scott.

The village is laid out around three squares linked by a long main street. The Duke's project had limited success owing to the remoteness of the settlement, but he made sure that each cottage had an acre or two of ground so that the villagers could produce most of their own food.

In 1862 this sleepy settlement was linked to Edinburgh and Carlisle by the opening of the Border Union Railway. That lasted for just over a century before it fell victim to Dr Beeching's cuts. The last train passing through was the night sleeper on 6 January 1969. Despite local protestors temporarily stopping the train by standing on the level crossing, the journey was completed, the line was closed, the track was lifted in 1970 and all the station buildings were demolished.

There are many stories and legends attached to the Armstrong Cross you will visit on this walk. One concerns the evil Lord De Soules, who reportedly molested a local girl. Her father challenged De Soules and was killed. A mob captured De Soules and were going to hang him when Alexander Armstrong, Laird of Mangerton, rescued him. To thank him De Soules invited him to dinner at Hermitage Castle and there had him murdered.

Another local legend has De Soules involved in black magic and as the perpetrator of many evil acts. Ultimately people rose against him, captured him and took him to the stone circle at Ninestane Rig where he was wrapped in a sheet of lead and boiled alive in a cauldron.

THE BASICS

Distance: 2½ miles / 4km

Gradient: A few gentle climbs but lots of flat walking

Severity: Moderate

Approx time to walk: 2 hrs

Stiles: three

Map: OS Explorer 324 (Liddesdale & Kershope Forest)

Path description: Pavement, stone and dirt tracks and footpaths, old railway trackbed

Start point: Douglas Square, Newcastleton (GR NY483875)

Parking: Car park in Douglas Square and parking on road (TD9 0QD)

Landscape: Pastures, woodland, valley

Dog friendly: Not good for dogs unless you can lift them over the stiles

Public toilets: Langholm Street

Nearest food: The Olive Tree (South Hermitage Street). Grapes and Liddesdale Hotels (Douglas Square). Copshaw Kitchen (just beyond Douglas Square on North Hermitage Street)

NEWCASTLETON WALK

1. Walk up Langholm Street, passing the village hall, fire station and public toilets. When you see the road ahead bending to the left just beyond a grey stone house, turn left in front of the house and along a lane passing another house.

2. Continue from here along the trackbed of the old railway, following yellow Newcastleton Paths way-markers. The path is well surfaced but can be muddy at points, particularly after periods of heavy rain, so stout shoes or boots are recommended. When you reach a crossroads with a track, turn right and head uphill through the woodlands of Boosie Plantation.

3. Although you will be climbing uphill, the gradient is gentle. Eventually you will come to a stile, just beyond a gate. This gate is easy to open if you wish to avoid the stile, but there are others where you don't have any options.

4. The track continues to climb to reach a junction with another path. Although a way-mark here indicates a left turn it is fairly obvious that the main track is turning left. As you continue along this track it gets steadily rougher. Have a look round about you to see if you can identify what were once hedgerows for a system of small fields. The fences have been largely abandoned and have grown into trees. Only the uniform lines indicate their former use. You'll come across a few, seemingly abandoned, agricultural implements along this section of the walk and a variety of wildflowers and trees. Look out for foxglove, Scotch thistle, beech trees and hawthorn in particular. Continue, past a gate, then cross a stile to the end of the track, then cross another stile and finally reach the end of the track where a way-marker indicates a right turn.

5. Follow the line of an ancient beech hedge. You will see the walls of the cemetery in front of you. Look out also for a way-marker on your left, then veer left, go downhill a short distance to cross a wooden footbridge and head uphill on the other side, passing another way-marker and ascending a series of steps to reach the cemetery wall.

6. Climb over the stile here and go right, then right again through a gap in the wall to get into the old part of the cemetery. Spend some time wandering around looking at the stones. There's an enclosure where some mediaeval stones or fragments have been preserved. The tall obelisk is a memorial to William Armstrong, a farmer at Sorbietrees, who was shot dead without warning in 1851 by the Revd Joseph Smith of

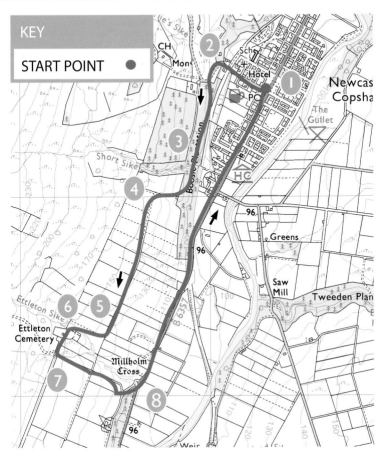

Cumberland. Another notable stone is that to the Revd John Black, parish minister for fifty years, who is described as 'a man of genius'.

7. At the top of the cemetery turn left to go through a kissing gate, then follow the access road as it heads downhill to reach the B6357. At the bottom, near the road junction, turn left to visit the Milholm Cross. This is apparently the oldest relic of the Armstrong Clan and was erected in memory of one of their number who was killed at Hermitage Castle.

8. Turn left along the B6357. It's just a short section but keep an eye out for speeding cars. Just past the Newcastleton village sign, cross the road, turn left through a gate and continue along the old railway. When you reach the crossroads at point 2, turn right and return to the main road. Turn left and follow it back to Douglas Square.

ABOUT THE AUTHORS

Moira McCrossan and Hugh Taylor are a husband and wife writing team now specialising in travel for the over 50s and walking guides. They are also travel editors of the UK's premier over 50s website laterlife.com.

Moira McCrossan spent most of her working life in education and was a primary school head teacher. An active trade unionist, she is a former President of the Educational Institute of Scotland, and served on the General Council of the Scottish TUC and on the Women's National Commission, with whom she co-authored the report *Growing up Female in the UK*. She was also a contributor to the *Times Educational Supplement* (Scotland).

Hugh Taylor is an award-winning travel writer, broadcaster and photographer. He worked extensively for BBC Radio, producing several series for Radio 2 including *Doomsday in the Afternoon* about the music of the Scottish Travellers.

Together they have written or contributed to over forty travel and outdoor guides, some of which have been translated into several languages. They range from major country guides covering Scotland, Lebanon and Jordan to walking books throughout the UK. Their work has appeared worldwide in publications as diverse as *The Times*, *Woman's Realm*, *Choice*, *The Herald*, *Interval World* and the *Glencairn Gazette*. They live in the picturesque southern Scottish village of Moniaive and in Capena, a hill town just north of Rome.

The authors would like to thank Kimberley Keay of The Camping and Caravan Club, for providing our accommodation and the wardens and staff at the Club Sites in Lauder and Jedburgh for all their advice and help.